CHRIST IN CONTEMPORARY THOUGHT

THEMES FOR TODAY
James O'Gara, General Editor

CHRIST IN CONTEMPORARY THOUGHT

WILLIAM E. MAY

1970
PFLAUM, DAYTON, OHIO

Library of Congress Catalog Card Number: 79-133404
Pflaum/Standard
38 West Fifth Street
Dayton, Ohio 45402

Printed in the United States of America

ISBN 0-8278-9207-1
T5M1170/2M273

CONTENTS

Acknowledgments

The author wishes to thank those who granted permission to use the following:

Excerpts from *The Jerusalem Bible,* copyright © 1966 by Darton, Longman & Todd, Ltd. of London, and Doubleday & Company, Inc. of New York. Used with the permission of the publishers.

Excerpts from *Jesus—God and Man* by Wolfhart Pannenberg. Copyright © MCMLXVIII, The Westminster Press. Used with the permission of the publishers, The Westminster Press of Philadelphia, and SCM Press of London.

Excerpts from *The Christology of the New Testament* (Revised Edition) by Oscar Cullman. Translated by Shirley C. Guthrie and Charles A. M. Hall. Published in the U.S.A. by The Westminster Press, 1964. © SCM Press, Ltd., 1959, 1963. Used with the permission of the publishers, The Westminster Press of Philadelphia, and SCM Press of London.

Excerpts from *The Evangelical Theology: An Introduction* by Karl Barth. Used with the permission of the publisher, Holt, Rinehart and Winston of New York.

Excerpts from *A New Quest of the Historical Jesus* by James M. Robinson. Used with the permission of the publisher, SCM Press of London.

Introduction

The following pages are intended to serve as a report on the various ways in which some twentieth-century theologians seek to approach the mystery of Christ. The Christian faith is by no means a cerebral activity; rather, it is a way of life, a commitment to persons, a call to action, a challenge to become involved and to risk one's life. But it is all this because it is first and foremost a movement rooted in, centered on, and sustained in being by Jesus of Nazareth, the Christ of God. Thus Christians of every age have been concerned to "know" their Lord, to follow his invitation to discipleship, to become one with him. And this kind of "knowing" is attained principally by "doing": by loving Jesus as he told us he should be loved — in our fellowmen.

The theologians whose views we shall examine realize all this, but they are convinced that the living, experiential dimensions of the Christian faith can be deepened and made to take on a new vitality if the reality of Jesus' person and work is illuminated to the fullest extent possible. Believers, they are convinced, not only want to know Jesus in the sense described above but also to know *about* him; they want to know who he was and who he is and why he is called Lord, Savior, Redeemer, Son of God, God. Because Jesus is unfathomable, this urge to know more and more about him can never be quenched, can never reach its end. Yet, Christians of every generation feel compelled to continue their search for understanding because they realize that understanding generates and supports their love for and dedication to Jesus.

Readers will find a wide range of approaches to and opinions about Jesus reflected in this report. The positions discussed have been chosen first of all with a view to offering readers a representative sampling of what major twentieth-century theologians have to say about Jesus. But more importantly they were chosen because they strike this reporter as being significant, stimulating, challenging, creative, and at times truly exciting in virtue of the new horizons they disclose and the fresh perspectives they offer for understanding who Jesus is and why millions of human beings have found in him their lord and savior. Obviously this does not imply agreement with all the positions described in this report; it would be an impossible contradiction, for example, to accept simultaneously the Jesus emerging from the writings of Paul Tillich and the Christ portrayed by Karl Barth. Yet, I am convinced that all of the theologians whose views are recorded here have something important to say to us about Jesus and about ourselves. At times what they have to say is unsettling and disturbing, but by this very fact they compel us to stop short and to search ourselves in order to see just what we do believe.

I have tried to record the positions taken as accurately as possible. Because I am not a professional theologian, I have sought to highlight those features of contemporary thought about Jesus that can be appreciated by the questioning believer and to leave for trained theologians a discussion of those elements that seem to require a more formal theological background in order to be understood. My hope has been to communicate something of the urgency and relevancy that twentieth-century theologians have contributed to our understanding of the mystery of Jesus, to show how they have seen the significance of Jesus and the meaning of man as interlocking, interpenetrating issues, each shedding light on the other. It is with this hope that I leave the value of this book in the hands of its readers who can judge its merits on the measure of its success in fulfilling this hope.

1. The Old and The New Christology

"Who do people say I am?" was the question that Jesus put before his disciples shortly before he went to Jerusalem to suffer his passion and death (Mark 8, 27). Many answers can be given to this question, and Mark immediately lists several that were current at the time: John the Baptist, Elijah, or another one of the prophets. To these answers can be added all those that have been offered by ancient and modern historical research, philosophy, and other sciences. Jesus of Nazareth has been identified as an itinerant Jewish rabbi, the greatest ethical teacher of all time, a religious fanatic, a mythical projection of man's ineradicable desire to become divine, a deceiver, and a fool. Yet, it is important to note that all these answers are given to the question "Who do *people* say I am?" And all of these answers, although paradoxically they contain some elements of truth, miss the mark, simply because they are offered by those for whom Jesus is simply one human being among many — extraordinary perhaps, undoubtedly important and interesting, but in no way unique. In other words these answers to the question of Jesus' identity come from those who do not believe in Jesus, who are not convinced that in some way or another Jesus is the center of human history, the living embodiment of God's love for men.

But Jesus put another question to his disciples that day. He asked them "But you, who do *you* say I am?" Now he is asking his disciples, that is, those who believe in him, who are committed to him in a personal way, to state their own convictions about him and to express why they have put their faith in him.[1] Peter, speaking for Jesus' first disciples and for all the generations of the faithful to follow, replied: "You are the Christ, the Son of the living God" (Matthew 16, 17). Peter's answer, as the gospel makes clear, can only be given on the basis of faith. Christians of every age are called upon to make their own personal response to this question, and throughout this book we will be concerned with the replies provided by leading representative Christian theologians of our own day. For our age, just as every preceding age of the Christian people, has its own culture, its own historical setting, its own world view; and all these factors in some way must condition the nature of our response to the question, "Who do *you* say that I am?" Thus our response is not, and cannot be, entirely the same as that of Peter or of the Nicene Fathers or of the medieval Church or of our nineteenth-century forebears.

Yet, our response cannot be entirely different either, because there are certain constants running through the Christian tradition that are clearly recognizable in every age, despite divergencies of interest and emphasis and formulation. These constants can be summed up by saying that Christians always have acknowledged that the man Jesus of Nazareth is Son of God, Incarnate Word, the definitive revelation of the Father, the mediator between God and man, our redeemer. The Church has always vigorously guarded against three pitfalls: to deny Jesus'

2

true divinity, to deny his true humanity, and to make Jesus' humanity and divinity two separate and juxtaposed realities instead of one irreducible unity. The constant factors or essential elements running through the entire history of Christian belief in Jesus have been ably summed up recently by an Anglican theologian, Norman Pittenger, and it will be useful to see how he states this tradition, inasmuch as his statement will provide us with some criteria for assessing the value of some of the views to be presented later. Pittenger writes:

> First, there is the firm conviction that in some fashion we meet God in the event of Jesus Christ. Second, there is the equally firm conviction that God is thus met in a genuine, historically conditioned, and entirely human being. Third, there is the assurance that God, met in this man, and the man in whom God is met, are in relationship one with the other, in a manner or mode which is neither accidental nor incidental but the most complete interpenetration — and this means that the relationship or the union . . . must be conceived after the analogy of personal union. [2]

It takes only a little reflection to see that the constants or essential elements summarized by Pittenger accurately reflect the teachings familiar to all of us when we recite the Apostles' Creed and the Nicene Creed.[3] These *are* the constantly voiced convictions of the Christian community about Jesus of Nazareth: that he is true man, that he is true God, that the man Jesus is personally united to or, better, one with God.

Yet, there has always been a tension within the Christian community in holding all of these truths together, in affirming them all simultaneously and meaningfully. This tension arose very early in the Christian Church and, somewhat paradoxically, the initial difficulties centered on the humanity of Jesus, for there is no doubt that certain passages in the epistles of John were directly aimed at an early Christian heretical sect that denied the real manhood of Jesus, making his humanity an empty show, a mask veiling his divinity.[4] Technically known as *docetism* (from a Greek verb meaning "to seem," and implying that Jesus was not truly a man but merely *seemed* to be a man), this is a particularly insidious attitude because it seemingly preserves the outward semblance of Christian faith (we encounter God in a unique way in Jesus) while eroding its substance. In addition a docetist mentality apparently has a peculiar attraction for Christian believers; and, as we shall soon see, it is a desire to eradicate this mentality that is a dominant operative factor in contemporary theology, in particular Catholic theology. That it has been a perennial threat to Christian believers becomes evident if we compare two statements by early Christian fathers. For instance we find Ignatius of Antioch, on his way to martyrdom, warning his fellow Christians against this mentality, passionately proclaiming:

> Be deaf . . . when anyone speaks to you apart from Jesus Christ, who was of the family of David, and of Mary, who was truly born, both ate and drank, was truly persecuted under Pontius Pilate, was truly crucified and died in the sight of those in heaven and on earth and under the earth . . . But if, as some affirm who are without God — that is, are unbelievers — his suffering was only a semblance . . . why am I a prisoner, and why do I even long to fight with the beasts? In that case I am dying in vain.[5]

Obviously what Ignatius, who died in A.D. 107, wanted to attack in this passionate cry was the view that Jesus was only apparently a man and that in reality he had no need of food and drink and that he really did not suffer an agonizing death. Yet, at the end of the second century, we find a great Father of the early Church, Clement of

Alexandria, suggesting that, because the Word of God was in Christ, he had no real need of food as we do, nor did he suffer or rejoice as we do, since Clement wrote:

> For he ate, not for the sake of the body, which was kept together by a holy energy, but in order that it might not enter into the minds of those who were with him to entertain a different opinion of him . . . he was entirely impassible, inaccessible to any movement of feeling, either pleasure or pain.[6]

Certainly there is a great difference in the ways in which these two Christian saints view Jesus. Who more accurately reflects our own way of looking at Jesus, Ignatius or Clement? Obviously this is a question that can only be answered by reflecting on our own attitudes and spontaneous response. But it can, I believe, be said that the majority of contemporary theologians would side with Ignatius. To see why, we shall now examine some of the more important factors leading theologians today to rethink the Christian teaching on the mystery of Jesus. But first it may be helpful to sum up what in practice most of us who call ourselves Christians actually do believe about Jesus, because it is this widespread, practical understanding of Jesus that has in large measure prompted contemporary theologians to become more urgent in their endeavors to offer the public a somewhat different picture.

Previously we made a passing reference to the Apostles' and Nicene Creeds as handy, convenient expressions of the principal convictions about Jesus that are shared by those who call themselves Christians. Let us now look a bit more closely at the second of these, the Nicene Creed, to see what it tells us about Christ. Its influence in shaping on a practical level our attitudes about Jesus ought to be enormous, because it is, after all, the familiar profession of our faith that we make Sunday after Sunday at Mass. Precisely what do we affirm in this Creed? The passages pertinent to our belief in Jesus are the following:

> We believe in one Lord, Jesus Christ, the only Son of God, eternally begotten of the Father, God from God, Light from Light, true God from true God, begotten, not made, one in Being with the Father. Through him all things were made. For us men and for our salvation he came down from heaven; by the power of the Holy Spirit he was born of the Virgin Mary and became man. For our sake he was crucified under Pontius Pilate; he suffered, died, and was buried. On the third day he rose again from the dead in fulfillment of the Scriptures. He ascended into heaven and is seated at the right hand of the Father. He will come again in glory to judge the living and the dead, and his kingdom will have no end.

As we indicated earlier, this confession contains all the basic elements of the mystery of Christ: he is truly both God and man; he suffered a real death at a definite point in time; he rose from the dead and will come again. So far, so good, and I have no intention whatsoever to call into doubt any of the statements about Jesus affirmed in this time-honored and well-known profession of faith. Yet, it is instructive, I believe, to observe that in the Nicene Creed we first affirm Jesus' divinity and only afterwards do we speak about his humanity. Obviously an emphasis on the true divinity of Jesus was absolutely necessary at the time when this creedal profession was hammered out, for at that time, as Jerome tells us, "half the world awoke to find itself Arian." At that time the heresy of Arius, who denied the true Godhood of Jesus, had taken root everywhere throughout Christendom and in order to preserve intact and meaningfully the tradition passed on by the Apostles and their successors, the Fathers of Nicea and Constantinople[7] naturally found it necessary to affirm in no uncertain terms that Jesus was, unlike us, not an "adopted son" of God but the Father's natural Son, that he was truly God, and that in Jesus *God had truly become man*. Just as obviously, throughout the history of the Christian Church, it has been necessary to affirm again and again, against those who have held that Jesus is merely man, albeit an unusually important and extraordinary one, that Jesus is truly divine. Yet, it can, I believe, be justly said, as a British Catholic theologian did say, that since the time of the Arian controversies of the fourth century "theologians have stepped on each other's heels to tell their fellow Christians that 'Jesus is God'."[8] The result, as might be expected, is that most of us tend to put a heavier emphasis on Jesus' divinity than on his humanity, and so great is this emphasis that many contemporary theologians fear that, on a popular level at least, the greatest threat to the Christian faith is a docetism. This may be unconscious and inarticulate and it may be combined with a vocal, at times vociferous, affirmation of Jesus' humanity. But, these theologians ask, do we really do justice to Jesus' full humanity? Do we really mean it when we say that Jesus was fully human?

If we add to the consideration that the Nicene Creed emphasizes the divinity of Jesus the fact that for most Catholics Jesus' own humanity has been presented in terms of scholastic philosophy and not in terms of biblical imagery, the force of contemporary theologians' uneasiness over our understanding of the mystery of Christ becomes more evident. De Rosa, I believe, accurately assesses the situation when he writes:

> During the Middle Ages the co-equality of Son and Father was to the fore in theological writing and discussion. Furthermore, an even stranger idea of what perfect manhood consisted in held sway among the mediaevals than was to be found [in patristic thinkers]. In the first instance, Adam

was credited with amazing privileges of mind and body. A fortiori, it was argued, Christ, the second Adam, was deemed to be more perfect still. ... There grew up . . . a theology of Christ which put him beyond all human efforts at identification and imitation. To him was attributed the beatific vision of his Father from his conception, and an angelic knowledge of the whole of human history. Such things were thought to be entailed by Christ's divinity: if Jesus was God, he must have had a perfect humanity.[9]

The picture of Jesus' manhood sketched in this description is, in very large measure, the one most popular in the Christian imagination. From the very beginning of his life, Jesus consciously knew exactly who he was and what was to happen to him, what kind of death would befall him and that he would rise victoriously. Most of us imagine that the man Jesus knew in detail the entire course of future history. Although the biblical data − which we shall examine at more length later − are not completely clear on the subject of the human consciousness of Jesus, they certainly provide a picture far different from the one just offered.[10] In addition it is difficult to see how this image of the man Jesus can be squared with another constant in the Christian tradition, namely that Jesus was fully a man, just as human as we are, like us perfectly in all things save sin.

In short, although we verbally affirm that Jesus is both God and man − or in the more precise terminology of the Council of Chalcedon,[11] that the one person, Jesus Christ, possessed fully a human and a divine nature − there is the danger that, particularly on a popular and imaginative level, we effectively deny Jesus' true manhood and conceive of his human nature as a pure instrument in the hands of the divine person. This point is effectively made by one of the most significant theologians of today, Karl Rahner, who writes:

> . . . if the human 'nature' of the doctrine of the Two Natures is seen merely *in the customary sense* of a pure 'instrument', the possessor of this instrument can no longer be thought of as Mediator. He would simply be Mediator to himself . . . this reduction of the Mediator to a mean term between God and man does exist in the common mind, when *nature* is seen as a mere instrument of the person, and consequently has no significance for a *divine* Person. . . . The almost unavoidable consequence of all this is a conception, which undoubtedly dominates the popular mind (without of course reaching the stage of consciously formulated heresy), and which could be put rather as follows: 'When our Lord (=God) walked on earth with his disciples, still humble and unrecognized'. . . . [12]

In other words, what many contemporary theologians find disturbing about the ordinary way of presenting the mystery of Jesus is simply the fact that "popular Christology has always been dominantly docetic. That is to say, Christ only appeared to be a man or looked like a man: 'underneath' he was God."[13] In short, "the traditional . . . way of describing the Incarnation almost invariably suggests that Jesus was really God almighty walking about on earth, dressed up as a man."[14]

Another reason why contemporary theologians are actively engaged in reformulating the traditional teaching about Jesus is rooted in a new understanding of scripture. Although, as Rahner and others have noted,[15] Catholic theology concerning the mystery of Christ has, until recently, been more scholastic than biblical in its approach, there would be a need for recasting the teaching even had its more traditional formulation been couched in biblical language. Biblical criticism of the past hundred years has changed to a considerable extent the way in which the scriptures and, in particular, the Gospels, are to be regarded as source materials. When most of us were in grade school, we — and our teachers — customarily looked on the Gospels as the simple reports of Jesus' immediate disciples of what Jesus did and said. Although we may not formally have regarded the Gospels as biographies in the modern sense, we were inclined to do so, and the various "lives" of Jesus popular among Catholics of a generation ago — Ricciotti's, Prat's, Grandmaison's — were in essence efforts to show how a consistent chronological framework could be worked out by comparing data from the different Gospels and how the sayings and actions attributed to Jesus by each of the evangelists could be fitted into this framework. In other words, the tendency was to assume that the Gospels were pretty straightforward narrative accounts of what had actually, historically happened during the course of Jesus' life. Consequently when we read the Gospel accounts of a particular incident in the life of Jesus or of a particular sermon or parable attributed to him, we assumed that the report was a faithful transcript of precisely what was done or said.

Today, however, we realize that this attitude toward the Gospels cannot be maintained. If we examine the Gospel accounts closely — and contemporary biblical scholars have subjected them to extremely minute analysis — they present some perplexing problems. An example may help make this clear, and for the purpose of illustration we can look at the various accounts of the Risen Jesus in the New Testament. The New Testament contains several reports of appearances of the Risen Lord. Matthew reports two: one to the women (Mary Magdalene and the "other Mary") near the empty tomb, and one to the Eleven on the "mountain" in Galilee (Matthew 28, 9-10, 16-20). Luke also has two appearances: one to two of the disciples on the road to Emmaus, and another to the Eleven and their companions in Jerusalem (Luke 24, 13-25, 36-53). John has four accounts: one to Mary Magdalene at the empty tomb, a second to the disciples without Thomas, a third to Thomas with the disciples, all three in Jerusalem (John 20, 14-18, 19-22, 24-29); the fourth took place in Galilee and begins with a miraculous catch of fish (John 21). Mark in 16, 1-8 tells of the visit of three women (Mary Magdalene, Mary the mother of James, and Salome) to the tomb, which they find empty; later, in 16, 9-20, he relates three appearances of the Risen Jesus: one to Mary Magdalene, one to two disciples along the road, and a third to the Eleven "at table." Although he does not specify the place, the context indicates that all three of these appearances took place in Jerusalem and vicinity. In addition, from Luke's account it seems that all the appearances took place on a single day, whereas John's Gospel and the first chapter of Acts — composed by the same Luke who wrote the Gospel! — speak of a longer period of time ("forty days" according to Acts). Finally, in his first letter to the Corinthians, Paul, in relating what he had been taught himself, speaks of appearances of the Risen Jesus "first to Cephas and secondly to the Twelve. Next he appeared to more than five hundred of the brothers . . . then he appeared to James, and then to all the apostles; and last of all he appeared to me" (1 Corinthians 15, 5-8).

From this brief resume of the pertinent texts we can see that one of the most serious problems is to reconcile the *places* where the appearances of the Risen Lord occurred. Were they in Galilee, Jerusalem, or both? Efforts to argue that each report should be taken at face value have, in the opinion of contemporary exegetes, proved a failure. As one scholar, Raymond E. Brown, has noted,

It is virtually an untenable thesis that Jesus appeared first to the Eleven in Jerusalem for about a week (John 20:26), and that afterwards they went to Galilee . . . where he appeared to them on the seashore (John 21) and on the mountain

11

(Matthew 28) and that finally they returned to Jerusalem where Jesus appeared to them before ascending (Acts 1). This sequence does violence to the Gospel evidence.[16]

Another problem centers on the empty tomb accounts, chiefly because they vary so widely in their details. As Brown observes: "it is extremely interesting to compare the accounts to find out whether there were one or two angels (young men), whether they were outside or inside the tomb, whether they were sitting or standing." He continues by saying that Matthew 28, 1-5, where the women are present when an angel comes down from heaven and opens the tomb, is totally at variance with the other accounts where the stone is already rolled back when the women arrive.[17]

As this example should make clear, the gospel accounts may indeed be historically reliable narratives, but they certainly cannot be regarded as biographies of Jesus in the way in which Ludwig's *Life of Napoleon* or Sandburg's volumes on Lincoln can be regarded as biographical. In fact, as contemporary biblical scholars maintain and as will be detailed at more length in the next chapter, the Gospels must be regarded as completely unique types of literature. They reflect the faith of the early Christian Church in the person of Jesus, and this faith reinterpreted and reevaluated events in the earthly life of Jesus in the light of the Easter faith in his resurrection from the dead and his installation as Risen Lord by God.[18] What is important from our perspective here is that theologians today, in reworking the Church's tradition about Jesus, must of necessity use the biblical data in a manner quite different from that of theologians of previous centuries. The impact of biblical research on the contemporary quest for understanding the mystery of Jesus has been exceptionally profound. More of this will be found in the next chapter.

A final factor at work among theologians today in their efforts to reformulate the teaching on Jesus centers on contemporary culture and the contemporary world view. The classical doctrine on the mystery of Jesus was formulated in a culture in which Greek philosophical concepts prevailed, particularly the concepts of person and nature. Many theologians and philosophers today, although there is by no means any unanimity here, believe that the metaphysical notions of person and nature, as predicated of Jesus in the formula of Chalcedon, are no longer intelligible to contemporary man.[19] Although it can be doubted whether some advocates of this point of view, e.g. the death-of-God theologians Hamilton and Altizer, have any real appreciation for or understanding of the genuine meaning of these metaphysical concepts, and argued that they reject them simply on the grounds that they are no longer "relevant" or meaningful for contemporary man,[20] it is apparent that these concepts have been given new meanings by contemporary philosophy and psychology and that this fact alone requires some kind of reworking of these notions when they are attributed to Jesus.

In addition and more importantly, contemporary theologians point out that the teaching of the Church about Jesus developed in a world that knew nothing of evolutionary theory. For the ancients and, indeed, for the majority of Christians until the very recent past, the world that Jesus came to redeem was pretty much the same world that had been created in the beginning by God. For them there had been no kind of evolution within the human race. Furthermore although the notion that man is a composite of body and soul is more properly a heritage from the Greeks than from the Hebrews from whom we derive the Bible, the idea that men are creatures of body and soul and that the soul is naturally immortal soon became widespread in Christianity, with important repercussions on the teaching about Jesus — as the treatises dealing with the manner of Jesus' infused knowledge and his activities of human knowing and willing testify. Whether this way of viewing man can be reconciled with contemporary evolutionary thought is a question that has loomed large in the minds of theologians. It is one of the major factors that helps to shape the contemporary way that theologians attempt to reformulate the teaching of the Church on the reality of Jesus.

These factors — an uneasiness with the traditional teaching, particularly on the popular level, for an overemphasis on the divinity of Jesus to a practical neglect of his humanity; a new way of using the biblical data as sources for understanding Jesus; and a world view colored by evolutionary theory and a new understanding of what it means to be a human being — have all been operative, to some extent, in the work of contemporary theologians. Naturally some factors predominate in some individual representatives of current Christological thought whereas in others a different factor is the more controlling. We shall see all this at work in the chapters to follow. Since the new understanding of scripture is, in fact, common to all contemporary theologians and has, in some ways at least, been the most important of all, it is to this that we shall first turn.

2. Jesus and Contemporary Biblical Scholarship

The principal sources for our knowledge about Jesus are the books of the New Testament, in particular the Gospels. In Chapter One we noted that one of the major factors compelling theologians today to reassess the traditional teaching about Jesus common among Christians was rooted in a new understanding of the nature of these writings. In this chapter we will seek to spell out the major developments of New Testament criticism insofar as they affect our understanding of Jesus. But before turning to these developments, it seems advisable first to offer a summary of the teaching about Jesus that we find in the New Testament itself.

The Gospels, of course, are the principal New Testament documents bearing witness to the person and work of Jesus. But Jesus and his mission are the subject of all the New Testament books; and we discover that the image of Jesus set forth in the epistles of Paul and in the Acts of the Apostles, for example, not only conforms to the Jesus we meet in the Gospels but also affords us additional insights into the meaning Jesus possessed for the earliest Christians. In fact a good way to see just how Jesus was viewed by his immediate disciples is to look at the preaching or proclamation about Jesus and his work that we find in the Acts of the Apostles. This preaching is well illustrated by the "sermon" that Peter delivered on the first Pentecost, and we find it reported in Acts 2, 22-36. The passage reads:

> 'Men of Israel, listen to what I am going to say: Jesus the Nazarene was a man commended to you by God by the miracles and portents and signs that God worked through him when he was among you. . . . This man, who was put into your power by the deliberate intention and foreknowledge of God, you took and had crucified by men outside the Law. You killed him, but God raised him to life, freeing him from the pangs of Hades; for it was impossible for him to be held in its power. . . he is the one who was *not abandoned to Hades.* and whose body did not *experience corruption.* God raised this man Jesus to life, and all of us are witnesses to that. Now raised to the heights by God's right hand, he has received from the Father the Holy Spirit, who was promised. . . .
>
> For this reason the whole House of Israel can be certain that God has made this Jesus whom you crucified both Lord and Christ.'

If we analyze this text, we find the following elements in the picture of Jesus sketched by Peter in his Pentecost speech to the Jews of Jerusalem: Jesus was (1) truly a man, one who had grown up in the Palestinian village of Nazareth, whose (2) divine mission to mankind had been sealed with signs and miracles. This true man, Jesus, was (3) crucified by the Romans ("men outside the law") at the instigation of his fellow Jews and with the foreknowledge of God. But this same man, Jesus, escaped death (the "pangs of Hades"), for (4) God raised him from the dead and Peter and his fellow apostles are witnesses to the Risen Jesus. Finally (5), as a result of his rising from the dead, the man Jesus has been made both "Lord and Christ" by the Father. In addition, although this is not clear from the portion of the text cited, the man Jesus fulfilled the scriptures of the Jewish people. For in a section of his sermon that we omitted in citing this passage, Peter referred to Psalm 16, 8-11, and insisted that the man Jesus was the one who had fulfilled David's words that God would not abandon his "holy one" to Hades nor allow him to experience corruption. And the significance of this citation from the Psalms would not have been missed by those to whom Peter delivered his first account of the "good news" that is Jesus.

Certain other features of Peter's sermon should be noted. Take the titles "Lord" and "Christ" that he applies to Jesus. The term "Lord" is significant, for it was the Greek word *kyrios* or "lord" that was used in the Greek translation of the Hebrew Bible to designate the God of the Hebrew people; although in this particular passage the title may possibly not be referring to Jesus' divinity, there is almost universal recognition among biblical scholars that this title, when attributed to Jesus in the New Testament, is ordinarily intended to signify that the lordship attributed exclusively to Yahweh in the Old Testament is in some way the prerogative of Jesus.[1] The title "Christ," of course, is the Greek rendering of the Hebrew "Messiah" or God's "Anointed One." We should also note that in this sermon Peter seems to imply that Jesus "became" or "was made" both Lord and Christ because of his resurrection. Does this mean that prior to the resurrection Jesus was not the Christ, that he was not the Lord? As we shall soon see, this is a question of considerable significance in contemporary biblical studies.

The epistles of Paul are also important for showing us how the early Church looked upon Jesus. His letters are chronologically earlier than the Gospels,[2] and thus his testimony is a good indication of how widespread and fixed was the teaching about Jesus in the early Church even before this teaching was recorded in the Gospels. What, then, does Paul tell us about Jesus? He tells us that Jesus was truly a man, born of a woman (Romans 1, 3; Galatians 1, 19); that he was descended from Abraham (Galatians 3, 16) and David (Romans 1, 3); that he was holy and sinless (1 Corinthians 11, 1), meek and gentle (2 Corinthians 10, 1); that he died on the cross (Galatians 1, 17) and rose again from the dead (1 Corinthians 15, 1 ff). Moreover, by affirming that "God in Christ was reconciling the world to himself" (2 Corinthians 5, 19), Paul said in effect that the Yahweh of the Hebrew Bible, who was conceived as a saving God operative within history, had definitively made his saving presence felt in the person of Jesus; that is, it is in Jesus that God reveals himself to men as their redeemer and savior.

In addition, of all New Testament authors, Paul uses the title "Christ" most frequently of Jesus; in fact in Paul this title becomes a proper name for the man of Nazareth, as it has remained throughout the Christian tradition.

Of particular importance for the future development of Christian teaching about Jesus are the great hymns to Christ that we find in Paul's letters. A passage from the epistle to the Philippians is a good example of these Christological hymns, which many scholars today believe to be early liturgical songs incorporated by Paul in his epistles.[3] The passage follows:

> His state was divine,
> yet he did not cling
> to his equality with God
> but emptied himself
> to assume the condition of a slave,
> and became as men are;
> and being as all men are,
> he was humbler yet,
> even to accepting death,

death on a cross.
But God raised him high
and gave him the name
which is above all other names
so that *all beings*
in the heavens, on earth and in the underworld,
should bend the knee at the name of Jesus
and that every tongue should acclaim
Jesus Christ as Lord,
to the glory of God the Father. (Philippians 2, 6-11)

Among the important teachings included in this text is the insistence that Jesus was preexistent, that is, that he did not begin to be when he was born of Mary but that he had existed from the beginning, in an equality with God. This theme of Jesus' preexistence, although stressed in the Gospel according to John, in particular in its Prologue (John 1, 1-18) and in the great "I am" passages (for example, John 8, 58: "I tell you most solemnly, before Abraham ever was, I Am"), is not clearly apparent in the Synoptic Gospels, although there are some passages from these Gospels that imply Jesus' preexistence, for instance the "I am sent" (Matthew 15, 24; Luke 4, 43) and the "I have come" (Matthew 5, 17; Mark 2, 17; Luke 5, 32) texts.

But what about the Gospels? What do they tell us about Jesus? They inform us that Jesus was born of a virgin (Matthew 2, 1 ff.; Luke 1, 5 ff.), that he spent his youth in Nazareth (Matthew 2, 23), that he began his public ministry when he was "about 30" (Luke 3, 13), that he was baptized by John (Matthew 4, 1-11) and began his public life as a proclaimer of God's imminent reign in Galilee, using the town of Capernaum as the center of his operations (Matthew 4, 13). They tell us that at first he usually announced his message of God's love and presence in the synagogues of the Galilean villages (Matthew

4, 23; Mark 1, 21; Luke 4, 16), but that possibly because his message antagonized the Scribes and the Pharisees, he then preached in the open air, on hilltops (Matthew 5-7, the Sermon on the Mount), on the plains (Luke 6, 26-49), or from the fishing boats of his disciples (Mark 3, 7-12).

Jesus, the Gospels inform us, was one who spoke with authority, at times contrasting what had been said "of old" with what he had to say (Matthew 5-7); he proclaimed the fatherhood of God (Matthew 5, 45) and the need for making our moral conduct a matter of the heart, of internal assent (Matthew 5, 22). He taught that love, love even of enemies, is the way to express our love of God (Matthew 5, 44); and he confirmed his teaching with miracles and signs — the curing of the lame and deaf and blind, the raising of the dead, the forgiving of sinners. He was regarded by those who heard him as a prophet (Matthew 16, 14; Mark 6, 15) and as one who could read hearts (Matthew 9, 3; John 1, 45-50), an act ascribed in the Old Testament (Jeremiah 17, 9 f.) only to God.

The central theme of Jesus' teaching was the kingdom or reign of God.[4] This reign is present in the person of Jesus, but it will be realized fully in a future reign still to come (Matthew 18, 23-35). The meaning of God's reign is brought out in the parables, which show us that this reign of God is not imposed upon men from without but is a reign that they are invited to accept by a conversion of heart and a readiness to surrender totally to the demands of God.

Jesus was recognized by his disciples as the Messiah (Mark 8, 29; Matthew 16, 17-20; Luke 9, 18-21), but, quite possibly because the popular notion of the Messiah current among the Jews, who viewed this figure as a military hero who would restore the Davidic Kingdom and drive out the Romans, was at odds with his own understanding of messiahship, Jesus forbade his disciples to announce him as the Messiah to others.[5] Seemingly he preferred to call himself the "Son of Man"[6] and he was recognized by his disciples as the suffering servant portrayed in Isaiah.[7]

Finally the Gospels tell us that Jesus, after predicting his suffering and death, went to Jerusalem for the last time. There he had a final meal with his apostles, leaving them as a parting gift the eucharistic bread and wine. He was betrayed by one of his own into the hands of his enemies, and finally he was crucified by the Romans at the insistence of his enemies. But the Gospels insist that this was not the end; for after three days Jesus rose from the dead and was seen by his apostles — by Peter, James, John, and the others — and by the "doubting" Thomas, who after fingering the hands and the side of Jesus is led to confess, "My Lord and my God!" (John 20:28).

The image of Jesus given us throughout the New Testament, consequently, has a general consistency and includes or, perhaps better, foreshadows all those aspects of the mystery of Jesus that have been the concern of Christians of every generation. Is not this image definitive for all time? Is it not a sketch of Jesus' person and mission set in writing by his immediate followers and, consequently, a factual account that we must either accept or reject? These questions lead us to consider the developments in biblical scholarship during the past century or so, to see precisely why they have had such a tremendous impact on the way in which we evaluate the testimony of the New Testament.

The Jesus of History and the Christ of Faith

In Chapter One we called attention to the various discrepancies that are found in the New Testament accounts of the empty tomb. We did so to illustrate why contemporary biblical scholars have found it necessary to reexamine in a very critical way the exact nature of the New Testament narratives. Naturally the divergences in the details of the empty tomb story were noticed by earlier generations of Christians. And there were other discrepancies as well; for instance, according to the Synoptic Gospels, Jesus went up to Jerusalem to celebrate the Pasch only once, and the implication is that his ministry lasted only one year, whereas in John we read that Jesus celebrated the Pasch at least three times in Jerusalem. All of these puzzling elements in the Gospel narratives were, of course, apparent to readers of the New Testament prior to the rise of what is now known as biblical criticism. Every perceptive Christian recognized that there was a need to harmonize the four Gospels, as the publication of Gospel harmonies from the days of Tatian in 170 A.D. to the present indicates. Moreover many of the Fathers of the Church dealt extensively with the minor differences in the Gospel narratives; we may mention Origen, Jerome, and Augustine in particular. Nevertheless, until quite recently the discrepancies observed within the narratives were considered as relatively minor, as puzzling pieces in a mosaic that could ultimately be harmonized completely.

Above all, earlier generations of Christians were convinced, chiefly on the basis of testimony handed down from second-century Christian writers such as Papias, that two of the evangelists (Matthew and John) had themselves been numbered among the original disciples of Jesus and consequently were eyewitnesses to the events recorded in their Gospels. The authors of the other two Gospels were considered intimate associates of apostles — Mark, in this tradition, was Peter's helper and in his Gospel sought to set forth the remembrances that Peter had about his Lord, whereas Luke was identified with

Paul's "dear friend, the doctor" (Colossians 4, 14). Furthermore it was believed that Matthew's Gospel, which had originally been composed, according to Papias, in "the Hebrew [that is, the Aramaic] tongue," was the first of the Gospels to be written, and by many of the Church Fathers, for example St. Augustine, Mark's Gospel was regarded more or less as a condensed or abridged version of Matthew's. When we add to all these factors the consideration that earlier generations of Christians were more interested in the teaching set forth in the Gospels than in questions touching on their history and literary composition, we can realize why the problems illustrated by the differing empty tomb accounts were not regarded as exceptionally important. Today, however, things are much different. Let us now see why.

A brilliant phrase, coined in 1910 by an English scholar, William Montgomery, when confronted with translating an important study by Albert Schweitzer, puts the problem into focus immediately. The German title of Schweitzer's book was deadly dull and to the uninitiated completely uninformative, for it was called, literally, ''From Reimarus to Wrede.''[8] The English title is *The Quest of the Historical Jesus;* the story it tells and more particularly the movements to which this story gave rise are fascinating and will occupy our attention for the next several pages.

Herman Samuel Reimarus (1694-1768), the first person mentioned in the German title of Schweitzer's famous book, was a rationalist deist who sought to present Jesus as a historical person, freed from all dogmatic preoccupations. In fragments of a work of his published posthumously in 1778,[9] the historical Jesus is described as a Jewish revolutionary, a zealot, who failed in his efforts to usher in a messianic age. To this historical Jesus, Reimarus contrasts the Christ found in the Gospels and preached by the Church, whom he considered a deception fabricated by the disciples who, disappointed that their hopes for a restoration of a Davidic kingdom had been dashed to the ground by the crucifixion of their leader, stole the body of Jesus from the tomb and invented the stories of the resurrection and the second coming.

Although no one seriously holds Reimarus' position today and although it is a view repugnant to the Christian faithful, his distinction between the Jesus of history and the Christ of faith is one that has been operative in many believing Christians, in particular the Protestant biblical theologians of the nineteenth and early twentieth centuries. During the nineteenth century, there was a preoccupation with the problems of historiography, and this preoccupation influenced biblical scholarship greatly. Faced with the challenge that Reimarus had raised with this distinction, a whole generation of Protestant exegetes set out on a quest for the "Jesus of history" or the "historical Jesus." They did so because they were convinced that they could provide a solid basis for Christian belief only by showing that the Gospel narratives contained a nucleus of genuine historicity. In addition — and this is an important point to note — for these scholars the adjective "historical" in the expression "historical Jesus" had a very specialized meaning. This term was used, as James M. Robinson observes, "in the sense of 'things in the past which have been established by objective scholarship.' Consequently the expression 'historical Jesus' comes to mean: 'What can be known of Jesus of Nazareth by means of the scientific methods of the historian.' "[10]

With this understanding of their task, the nineteenth-century scholars considered it essential to sift the available sources, in this case the Gospels, in order to discover in them material that could be used in a scientifically historical manner in order to reconstruct the life of Christ. In evaluating the Gospels as source material for this kind of a "life of Jesus," they soon decided to discount the Gospel according to John, inasmuch as they regarded it as a purely theological interpretation of the ministry of Jesus and of little historical worth.[11] Because among other reasons so many passages in Mark are also found in Matthew and Luke, the scholars soon came to the conclusion that of all the Synoptic Gospels Mark offered the best promise for serving as a historical source. In fact by the end of the nineteenth century, there was general agreement that Mark's Gospel was the first of the written Gospels and that the Marcan account of Jesus' ministry had served as a general framework for those of Matthew and Luke. In addition these scholars postulated another source for the material found in Matthew and Luke. This hypothetical source, called Q (from the German word *Quelle,* source), was considered a collection of the sayings (parables, sermons, discourses, et cetera) attributed to Jesus. For these nineteenth-century scholars, consequently, the Gospel according the Mark offered the basic outline of Jesus' public life, while the Q source gave the earliest version of his teaching. It was on the basis of these "sources," Mark and the hypothetical Q, that various "lives" of Jesus were constructed during the course of the nineteenth century. The results, however, were rather meager, inasmuch as the Jesus emerging from these lives was a Jesus drawn in colors taken from the theological palettes of the scholars involved. One contemporary author puts it as follows:

> The "liberals" tended to eliminate the miraculous element in the Gospels regardless of the sources in which they appeared . . . there were considerable differences between the individual "Lives" produced by scholars even of the same general tradition — a fact which suggests either that the sources were not adequate or that the scholars added too much of their own imaginings. Broadly speaking, the

liberal tradition, using Mark as a base, portrayed the ministry of Jesus as falling into two parts: a successful ministry in Galilee ("the Galilean springtime"), then a somber ministry in Jerusalem leading to the final confrontation and crucifixion. [12]

As we have seen, the primacy of the Gospel according to Mark and the existence of a collection of "sayings" (the Q source) were crucial presuppositions for those engaged in the nineteenth-century "quest." Gradually, however, scholars began to realize that none of the Gospel materials, Mark included, could serve as the basis for a "scientific" history of the life of Jesus of Nazareth. An important landmark in the development of biblical criticism on this point was the publication in 1892 of Martin Kähler's *The So-called Historical Jesus and the Historic, Biblical Christ*. [13] Kähler clearly recognized that the standards of modern scientific historiography make it impossible to write a scientific life of Jesus. The reason is simply that the Gospels, and whatever sources from which they derive, are not "scientific" documents. They are expressions of faith, of the faith of the early Christian community in the risen and glorified Jesus. They are in other words *kerygmatic* documents, that is, documents "proclaiming" or "heralding" Jesus as the redeemer of mankind. [14] To make his point clear, Kähler distinguished between *Jesus* and *Christ*, between what is "historical" and "historic." [15] Obviously Kähler's distinction is reminiscent of that made earlier by Reimarus, but the point here is that acceptance of Kähler's position makes a quest for the historical Jesus, in the sense in which the term "historical" was taken during the nineteenth century, virtually meaningless.

The death knell to the nineteenth-century quest was sounded in 1901 by Wilhelm Wrede (the second figure mentioned in the title of Schweitzer's book), who showed in his *Messianic Secret in the Gospels* [16] that Mark is just as much a theological interpretation of the ministry of Jesus as are the other Synoptic Gospels, and consequently that efforts to use Mark as a critical historical source for reconstructing the outline of Jesus' life are doomed to failure.

In short, we can say that the nineteenth-century "quest" was possible only on the supposition that "the oldest sources" — for instance the Gospel according to Mark — could be accepted "as the same kind of objective, positivistic historiography which the nineteenth century aspired to write." [17] Once it was realized that these sources could not be accepted in this way, the nineteenth-century quest came to an end.

What all of this shows us is that by the beginning of this century, there was a general recognition among biblical scholars that the books of the New Testament, the Gospels in particular, *were not intended* to serve as scientific histories. They were expressions of faith; and they can serve as primary sources for giving us a history of the faith current in the early Church, but they cannot be considered as scientific accounts of the life and work of Jesus. Consequently the basic question during the present century has been: To what degree has the Church's confession colored or shaped the image of Jesus presented in the New Testament? Has it so distorted the picture that we can never hope to know just who Jesus was, or has it faithfully communicated to believers the reality of Jesus of Nazareth?

Although there certainly is no unanimity among biblical scholars, it has been generally recognized, chiefly as a result of work done by exegetes like C.H. Dodd, [18] that the kerygma itself has a historical content. In fact a "new quest of the historical Jesus" has recently been undertaken, chiefly by German biblical scholars, which can in large measure be characterized as "an attempt to show that the kerygmatic portrait is a faithful representation of the historical Jesus."[19] In undertaking this quest, these German scholars — the chief representatives are Ernst Käsemann, Ernst Fuchs, Gunther Bornkamm, Hans Conzelmann, and Gerhard Ebeling — have approached the question of the "Jesus of history" with a new understanding of history. Earlier we noted that the scholars of the nineteenth century regarded history as a strictly postivistic, scientific study, giving a priority to chronological and geographical "facts," and concerned to recapture the past just as it happened. For scholars today this notion of history is no longer viable. As Robinson puts the matter:

The reason for this change does not lie in any restriction of the historical-critical method in dealing with the objective data, as if there were one group of historical facts accessible to historiography, while other historical facts were in principle beyond the historian's reach. Rather we have come to recognize that the objective factual level upon which the nineteenth century operated is only one dimension of history, and that a whole new dimension in the facts, a deeper and more central plane of meaning, had been largely bypassed. The nineteenth century saw the reality of the 'historical facts' as consisting largely in names, places, dates, occurrences, sequences, causes, effects — things which fall far short of being the actuality of history, if one understands by history the distinctively human, creative, unique, purposeful, which distinguishes man from nature. The dimension in which man actually exists, his 'world', the stance or outlook from which he acts, his understanding of his existence behind what he does, the way he meets his basic programs and the answer his life implies to the human dilemma, the significance he had as the environment of those who knew him, the continuing history his life produces, the possibility of existence which his life presents to me as an alternative — such matters as these have become central in an attempt to understand history. It is this deeper level of of the reality of 'Jesus of Nazareth as he actually was' which was not reached by 'the reconstruction of his biography by means of objective historical method.'[20]

Although the results of the "new quest," as set forth in the works of the German scholars mentioned previously, have been relatively meager, this direction in contemporary biblical thought shows that today biblical scholars are much more willing to see genuine historical truth in the biblical narratives than were the more positivistically minded critics of the previous century. Moreover, as one perceptive scholar, Raymond Brown, has pointed out, the quest undertaken by contemporary German scholars is not free of all presuppositions, and these presuppositions may be the root cause of the relatively meager results. Chief among these presuppositions are the following: first, "an existentialist preoccupation," which makes the scholars involved concentrate perhaps too excessively on the meaning that Jesus of Nazareth has for our own personal existence to the detriment of interest in the factual details of his life; second, a methodological approach which is inclined to be minimalist — that is, the scholars tend to restrict "authentic" historical material to biblical passages that certainly cannot be regarded as inauthentic, whereas, as Brown notes, "it would seem logical . . . that authenticity would be the general presumption, and lack of authenticity the exception," unless it could be shown that the Gospels were written primarily to de-deceive. Third, there is a failure to take the Gospel of John seriously.[21] Nevertheless, contemporary biblical scholars are coming to a realization that the kerygmatic proclamation of Jesus in the Gospels, while admittedly affected by the faith of the Church in the risen Jesus, is substantially authentic.

Form Criticism

Before going on in the concluding sections of this chapter to consider the christology found in the writings of two representative contemporary biblical theologians, Rudolf Bultmann and Oscar Cullmann, some observations about "form criticism" are in order, inasmuch as this way of looking at the Gospel materials is generally accepted by biblical scholars as a useful tool for understanding the kind of literature that the New Testament is. Naturally there are many differences, at times quite substantial, in the way in which different biblical scholars use the "form critical" method, and the use of this method in no way indicates that the scholar necessarily accepts the philosophical presuppositions underlying the presentation in this method in the works of its principal exponents, Martin Dibelius and Rudolf Bultmann. Still it is regarded as a valuable tool of Gospel research for shedding light on the precise character of the various kinds of narratives and dialogues that we find in the Gospels.

Actually a literary form is simply a part of the communication of meaning. A word or a sentence taken by itself and out of context does not have its full meaning; and the literary form in which they are found provides us with the immediate context for understanding the meaning of words and sentences. John L. McKenzie tells us:

> Diversity of literary forms arises because of a desire to deal with different subjects in a more meaningful way and to express different conceptions of a truth which is too large for expression through a single form. A single event, for instance, may be the subject of a prose narrative, a ballad or an epic poem, a tragedy, an oration, a philosophical reflection, and a prayer of lamentation or thanksgiving. Such diversity is possible only because the event can be conceived and represented in so many different ways. The 'mean-

ing' of the event lies not in its bare reality, but in the diversity of conceptions which it originates.[22]

Although the study of literary forms had been applied to classical literature for a long time, it was not extended to the books of the Old and New Testaments until relatively recent times. When it was so extended, scholars quickly came to the recognition that the biblical books, the Gospels included, provide us with a wide variety of such forms. In addition scholars gradually came to realize that there was a long history of oral tradition behind the written Gospels. In fact we began our brief summary of the New Testament teaching on Jesus by taking a sermon of Peter recorded in the Acts of the Apostles as a good summary of what that teaching was. Scholars today in general maintain that the speeches recorded in the Acts of the Apostles reflect in a rather accurate way the nature of the oral tradition that preceded the written composition of the Gospels.

But oral tradition, unlike a written book, is not capable of the sustained length characteristic of books. What it does do is to collect "smaller units, whether songs, stories, or other forms, and groups them around a person or place."[23] Oral tradition, precisely because it must be repeated over and over again in different circumstances, is likewise subject to constant revision; it is conceived and expressed anew in each generation.

What does this mean if we are to regard the written Gospels as the terminating point of a long history of oral tradition? It means that the full significance of a Gospel passage will not be seen until we have traced, as accurately as possible, the various stages through which it has gone until it attained the form in which we find it in the New Testament today. What form criticism has done in brief is to give us a new picture of the kind of literature that we are dealing with when we read the Gospel narratives. According to this way of looking at the biblical materials, the Gospel accounts can be analyzed into separate units, which in turn can be classified according to their forms as miracle stories, personal proclamations (the "I" sayings of Jesus), proverbs, parables, and so forth. These separate units were formulated in the early Christian community to meet its various needs — liturgical, apologetical, devotional, and so forth — and later on they were assembled and collected together, "like beads on a thread," as one contemporary author puts it,[24] to make up the written Gospels. In short what form criticism has done is to give us a picture of the written Gospels that, in a very large measure, confirms the reasons why the nineteenth-century quest for constructing a scientific biography of Jesus was an example of misdirected energy. For it follows, if the form critical method is accepted, that the written Gospels primarily and directly tell us about the early Christian community and its beliefs and only secondarily and indirectly provide us with "biographical" facts about the one in whom this community believed, Jesus of Nazareth.

Jesus in the Thought of Rudolf Bultmann

Rudolf Bultmann (1884-   ) is without doubt the biblical scholar whose conclusions regarding the nature of the Gospels and the significance of Jesus have aroused the most widespread attention and been the source of the most heated debates in this century. Frequently his thought has been characterized mainly as an endeavor to "demythologize" the Gospels, and in the popular mind this has usually been regarded as the removal from the Gospels of any elements smacking of the "supernatural" or "miraculous" and the consequent emasculation of the Christian faith. This, as we shall see, is a very one-sided and distorted way of presenting his views, in fact a caricature, although there are some elements of truth contained in this more or less popular understanding of Bultmann's work.

To understand what Bultmann is trying to do, we should realize first of all that he began his research into the New Testament when theology, particularly in Germany, was still under the influence of the liberal and rationalistic Protestantism of the nineteenth century, a mentality illustrated, as we have seen, in the efforts to reconstruct a scientific history of the life of Jesus. Bultmann was convinced that efforts of this nature were not only misdirected from the perspective of scholarly research but also that they failed miserably to convey the meaning of Jesus and of Christianity. In his eyes these attempts to discover the essence by Christianity by focussing on the personality of Jesus were completely rationalistic and alien to the meaning of faith in the person of Jesus. For the personality of Jesus — and by personality Bultmann means his empirically observable character, the complex of all the social and biographical data that can be accumulated concerning him — although the most exalted in the entire history of the world, was still only a *human* phenomenon, whereas the New Testament proclaims Jesus as the living Word of God speaking to men in the depths of their being. And Jesus, as this living Word, cannot be discovered by scientific research but only by faith itself.[25] As Bultmann sees it, it is not the personality or character of Jesus that is offered to men as an object of belief in the New Testament, but the "fact of his person" as the bearer of God's Word, so that to deny the messenger is to reject a message from God himself.[26] Consequently for Bultmann the Christology of the New Testament is not some kind of abstract metaphysical speculation about the identity of some heavenly being but is the very person of Jesus, his "here and now" character, his event, his mission, his summoning of men to answer the Word of God.[27]

Because he believes that concern for the human personality of Jesus is a rationalistic temptation against Christian faith and because his attention is primarily focussed on the "person" of Jesus, that is, his existential significance, it is quite true that Bultmann tends to put little emphasis on the actual historicity of Jesus of Nazareth, and in fact manifests a skepticism regarding the figure of Jesus as a historical person. For instance, we find him saying that "we can now know almost nothing concerning the life and personality of Jesus."[28] He holds that the person of Jesus "was mythologized from the very beginnings of earliest Christianity,"[29] and he is somewhat indifferent about knowing whether or not Jesus himself personally claimed to be the Messiah. Bultmann himself maintains that the historical Jesus did not make this claim, but the important point for us to note here is Bultmann's indifference to the question. He really does not care about questions of this kind, holding that "whether Jesus believed himself to be the Messiah or not is neither here nor there. If he did, that would only mean that he understood the decisive character of his work in the language peculiar to a contemporaneous Jewish image."[30] Consequently Bultmann is, as a biblical theologian, indifferent to the question of the "historical Jesus." But this does not mean that he denies any kind of continuity between the Jesus of history and the Christ of faith, for he acknowledges that the New Testament presents the Christ of faith as "a concrete figure of history – Jesus of Nazareth. His life is more than a mythical event; it is a human life which ended in the tragedy of crucifixion," and he acknowledges that "the New Testament claims that this Jesus of history, whose father and mother were well known

. . . is at the same time the pre-existent Son of God."[31]

Bultmann is known best, perhaps, as the advocate of the "demythologization" of the Gospels. Precisely what is this demythologization, and what does Bultmann mean by it? To see what this involves, we will investigate two major themes of critical significance in Bultmann's thought: (1) the kingdom or reign of God proclaimed by Jesus, and (2) the person of Jesus himself.

According to Bultmann, the original feature of Jesus' teaching about God was his radical notion of God's lordship over men: God is the one who completely dominates man's existence. In addition, and it is here that Bultmann sees the essential significance of the message of Jesus, the "eschatological" reign or kingdom of God actually begins with Jesus, with his here and now. This kingdom, which transcends the historical order, comes into being "not through the moral endeavor of men, but solely through the supernatural action of God. God will suddenly put an end to the world and to history, and He will bring in a new world, the world of eternal blessedness."[32] It was the proclamation of the initiation of this kingdom, Bultmann holds, that was the basic and central theme of Jesus' preaching. However, Bultmann adds, it is precisely the notion of the kingdom of God and the way in which this kingdom was announced that are among the "mythological" elements in the New Testament. According to Bultmann

The conception of a "Kingdom of God" is mythological, as is the conception of the eschatological drama. Just as mythological are the presuppositions of the expectation of Kingdom of God, namely, the theory that the world, although created by God, is ruled by the devil, Satan, and that his army, the demons, is the cause of all evil, sin and disease. The whole conception of the world which is presupposed in the preaching of Jesus as in the New Testament generally is mythological, i.e., the conception of the world as being structured in three stories, heaven, earth, and hell; the conception of the intervention of supernatural powers in the course of events; and the conception of miracles.[33]

Just as the notion of the eschatological kingdom of God is portrayed within the New Testament in mythological images, so too is the person of Jesus himself. In Bultmann's opinion the early Christian community pictured Jesus in mythological imagery, making him a supernatural being who would soon return as the Son of Man on the clouds of heaven to judge the world. The person of Jesus, Bultmann writes,

> is viewed in the light of mythology when he is said to have been begotten of the Holy Spirit and born of a virgin, and this becomes clearer still in Hellenistic Christian communities where he is understood to be the Son of God in a metaphysical sense, a great, pre-existent heavenly being who became man for the sake of our redemption and took on himself suffering, even the suffering of the cross.[34]

In addition we find in the New Testament all kinds of embellishments to this central story of Jesus. We encounter miracle narratives, voices from heaven, temptation by the devil, the casting out of evil spirits, and the like. Tales of this kind were quite believable in an age when people everywhere were under the impression that superhuman yet personal forces, both divine and demonic, were operative in the world and in human events. But they are not, Bultmann believes, credible for contemporary man. It is impossible, he says, "to use electric light and the wireless and to avail ourselves of modern medical and surgical discoveries and at the same time to believe in the New Testament world of demons and spirits."[35]

These and other features of the New Testament narratives — and among these other features Bultmann includes the story of the resurrection and the empty tomb[36] — are examples of mythological thought, or, as Bultmann describes it, "the use of imagery to express the otherworldly in terms of this world and the divine in terms of human life."[37] Moreover we must acknowledge that in determining what counts as mythological, Bultmann has equated "myth" with whatever conflicts with the contemporary scientific picture of the world. For him the world of the New Testament is mythological "because it is different from the conception of the world which has been formed and developed by science . . . and which has been accepted by all modern men."[38]

Nevertheless, because he is convinced that the central message of the New Testament is of permanent significance and that Jesus is truly the living Word of God, Bultmann believes that it is possible to disengage the meaning of the New Testament and to present it in a way that is meaningful and intelligible to contemporary man by means of the method of demythologizing. For him, demythologizing is a "hermeneutic method . . . a method of interpretation."[39] To demythologize the Gospel, moreover, is not for Bultmann to "rationalize" the Christian message. Here he emphatically declares that this is not at all the case and that on the contrary, "de-mythologizing makes clear the true meaning of God's mystery."[40] And in commenting further on this, Bultmann makes a significant admission, for he adds: "The incomprehensibility of God lies not in the sphere of theoretical thought but in the sphere of personal existence. Not what God is in himself, but how he acts with men, is the mystery in which faith is interested."[41] From this we can be quite certain that Bultmann's thought is of significance not for what he really is able to tell us about God and Jesus, but for the insights that he does provide into the human situation; and I believe that critics like Leopold Malevez are quite correct in their judgment that the basic weakness of Bultmann as a theologian is that he is simply not interested in questions about the meaning and nature of God in himself, but solely in the meaning that God possesses for human existence.[42]

In applying the method of demythologizing to the issues of the kingdom of God and the person of Jesus, Bultmann does indeed stress the existential significance of the Gospels, that is, their depths of meaning for our own personal existence; and in elucidating this existential significance, he freely uses the categories developed by the existentialist philosopher, Martin Heidegger.[43] Here, too, his chief concern is with the themes of the eschatological kingdom of God and the person of Jesus.

Although the eschatological elements in the proclamation of the kingdom of God, such as the image of the Son of Man coming on clouds of heaven, the end of human history in a final conflagration, and so forth, are in Bultmann's eyes purely mythic imagery in the message of Jesus, he finds this proclamation of the eschatological kingdom of tremendous existential significance. When the announcement of the imminence of God's kingdom and of the end of the world is viewed from the perspective of existential analysis, we see that it is intended to tell us that "this present world, the world in which we live our lives and make our plans, is not the only world; that this world is temporal and transitory; yes, that it is ultimately empty and unreal."[44] Moreover — and this Bultmann holds is clearly brought out in the New Testament itself — this world is empty "not only because it is transitory, but because men have turned it into a place in which evil spreads and sin rules. The end of the world, therefore, is the judgment of God . . . the eschatological preaching [therefore] . . . first and foremost calls men to responsibility to God and to repentance."[45] The eschatological preaching, in effect, makes men think deeply about the meaning of their own lives; it causes them to realize that each individual human being stands before the imminent end of his own death, and it reminds each of us that we must work out own history and assume responsibility for our own existence. "In every moment," says Bultmann, "slumbers the possibility of being the eschatological moment. You must awaken to it."[46] As John Macquarrie has observed, "When we understand it in this way, the eschatological teaching of the New Testament ceases to be merely a curious survival . . . . When they are transferred to the actual individual existence, the eschatological ideas recover something of their urgency."[47]

Applying existential interpretation in order to demythologize the picture of Jesus given to us in the New Testament, we discover that Jesus' significance lies in the fact that he is the address or call or summons of God to man. "In his person he embodies the demand for decision . . . . He *is* the summons to decision."[48] Writes Bultmann:

> The living word of God is not invented by the human spirit and by human sagacity; it rises up in history. Its origin is an historical event, by which the speaking of this Word, the preaching, is rendered authoritative and legitimate. This event is Jesus Christ . . . what God has done in Jesus Christ is not an historical fact which is capable of historical proof. The objectifying historian as such cannot see that an historical person (Jesus of Nazareth) is the eternal Logos, the Word . . . . According to the New Testament the decisive significance of Jesus Christ is that he – in his person, his coming, his passion, and his glorification – is the eschatological event.[49]

Although he is convinced that the resurrection is a myth and the stories of the empty tomb are legends, Bultmann gives the "primitive myth" of a dying and rising god[50] an existential significance. For him "the resurrection is nothing else than belief in the cross as salvific event . . . . The cross is not salvific event because it is Christ's cross: it is Christ's cross because it is salvific event."[51] This puzzling, paradoxical statement is intended, commentators on Bultmann assure us,[52] to stress the primacy of existential meaning over brute fact. This means that the true reality of the cross is its divine meaning, symbolized by the legend of the resurrection. Only if we personally experience the cross as an event shedding light on our own existence and summoning us to conversion and total dedication to God can we recognize that God was in Christ. In short, as Macquarrie puts it, "to say that Christ is God is not to make a metaphysical pronouncement about Christ's person but to declare one's own attitude toward him . . . . It is then God himself who addresses us through the crucified and risen Christ."[53]

For Bultmann, accordingly, the various titles attributed to Jesus in the New Testament — Lord, Christ, Son of God, et cetera — do not mean that Jesus is a divine person. In Bultmann's view the ancient Church went astray and, in fact, became rationalistic, when it interpreted the event that was Jesus in terms of Greek metaphysics. To him the formula "Christ is God is erroneous if God is understood to be something objectifiable, whether in the Arian manner or the Nicene, the orthodox or the liberal. It is correct if 'God' here means the event of God's deed."[54] There is not, then, another divine person alongside God, as though Jewish monotheism were now completed by belief in a second divine person. Christian faith for Bultmann does not consist in attributing a divine nature and divine person to Jesus but in acknowledging that in Christ God speaks to the depths of the human person.[55]

In the preceding pages we have sought to outline the basic elements in Bultmann's thought about Jesus and

Christianity. It should be obvious that his views are considerably at variance with the traditional way of conceiving Jesus. And, to be honest, we must admit that a good deal of what Bultmann rejects in the tradition is rejected fundamentally on the basis of a philosophical presupposition: miracles, an incarnate God, resurrection from the dead — these and other elements discovered in the New Testament — were believable in a prescientific age but are simply incredible for contemporary men. Nevertheless, "Bultmannian" cannot be regarded as another way of saying rationalistic. His effort to demythologize the New Testament is, as a Catholic exegete observed, "an honest effort to bring the religious value of the New Testament home to modern man,"[56] and contemporary exegetes are agreed in affirming that Bultmann has done biblical scholarship a service by stressing that the Gospel tradition was formed in the light of the Easter faith of the early Christian community and that as a result, many incidents, as reported in the written Gospels, are viewed in the reflected light of Jesus' glorification as risen Lord.

We shall now turn to a brief examination of the christological thought of another contemporary biblical scholar, Oscar Cullmann. Cullmann, like Bultmann, employs the form critical method, yet, as we shall discover, he vigorously disagrees with most of Bultmann's conclusions and, in particular, with the presuppositions that deeply affect the nature of Bultmann's research.

The Christology of Oscar Cullmann

Oscar Cullmann (1902-   ) is an exceptionally cautious and careful biblical theologian, and he is especially anxious to avoid reading into Scripture what he hopes to find there. He insists that the reader of the New Testament be willing to put aside his preconceptions and be ready to *listen* to what the text itself has to say, even "if it contradicts this or that philosophical conception of whose correctness we are convinced."[57] Although he makes use of the form critical method and recognizes its worth as a tool for understanding the meaning of the biblical narratives, he deplores the air of certainty and self-confidence that some practitioners of this art claim for their conclusions, warning that "we all ought to apply the soberest judgment in this respect and impose great caution upon ourselves. Above all, we ought to rid ourselves of the practice of measuring the critical sense of a New Testament exegete by the number of verdicts against genuine authenticity which he pronounces."[58]

Cullmann's own major contribution to biblical research lies in his notion of redemptive or salvation history. For Cullmann one of the distinctive characteristics of the Judeo-Christian tradition lies in its conception of time and history. The biblical mentality at the root of this tradition regards time after the analogy of a straight line, rather than a cyclic process, as time was conceived by the ancient civilizations of the Near East and by those shaped by Greco-Roman thought. To the writers of the biblical books, time is "going somewhere." This means that there is a thrust to redemptive or salvation history and that salvation is expected to occur at some point along this line of time. The events that take place in redemptive history are the self-revelation of God, and although these events are of the same general character as other historical events, they are the result of God's direct intervention into human history and, as such, can be seen only with the eyes of faith. The events making up the line that is redemptive history are the individual moments (which Cullmann calls, after a Greek term, *kairoi*) that correspond to unique, unrepeatable facts.[59] For Cullmann the difference between the Jewish and the Christian understanding of time is not found in their understanding of what time signifies — both communities agree that time has a redemptive aspect and a forward thrust — but in their placing of the midpoint of time, and by midpoint is understood the *turning point* in the history of redemption, not a chronological point midway between the beginning and the end. For the Jews this midpoint lies in the future, whereas for the Christians this midpoint has already arrived in the person of Jesus and in the historical events of his life, death, and resurrection. For Cullmann it was infinitely "easier to believe in the redemptive history as long as its mid-point was still placed, as in Judaism, in the eschatological future, that is, in a time that could be *only* the object of prophecy and not at the same time of historical confirmation." The faith asked of Christians is something "much more difficult" inasmuch as it requires them to believe that the Messiah has truly appeared among men.[60] It is for this reason that Cullmann regards docetism as the most dangerous christological heresy and the most subtle. For even if it is confessed that Jesus was truly man, that he really lived among us in the flesh, there is frequently a temptation to make a selection of the events recorded in the Gospels, taking some as normative for salvation and rejecting others. The great danger of docetism, Cullmann believes, is that in it "redemption is not a thing that occurs in time; it is an abstract teaching."[61] In his polemic against docetism, we can see in Cullmann a hostility toward Bultmann as well. For in striking out against docetism, Cullmann insists that the redemptive events culminating in Jesus are real historical events, not just a mythological process of salvation described in terms of a historical figure.

For Cullmann Jesus is *the* kairos, the decisive event in redemptive history. In fact for him Christology, or the science whose object is Christ, takes precedence over theology, the science whose object is God. He brings this point across by arguing as follows:

> Christology is usually considered as a sub-division of the-
> ology . . . . This arrangement is . . . encouraged by the order
> of the two articles God-Christ in the later confessions of
> faith. That order does in fact imply that the early Church
> was interested first of all in God and only then in Christ.
> But the unequal length of the two articles shows that this
> is not really the case . . . . [Moreover] the oldest confes-
> sions are . . . expressed exclusively in Christological terms
> . . . and connect Christ with creation.[62]

His point here is that we come to know who God is through
Jesus, who is the definitive revelation of God's redemptive love for mankind.

In approaching the subject of the significance of Jesus,
Cullmann follows what has been called a "functional"
approach. This approach seeks to discover who Jesus
is by discovering just what he has done for mankind, just
what function he fulfilled in the course of redemptive history. It is contrasted with what is called an "ontological"
or "metaphysical" approach, one concerned with questions dealing with the nature and person of Jesus. In Cullmann's view it is the functional approach that was taken
by the New Testament, whose teaching on Jesus was
conveyed primarily by attributing to him various titles,
each signifying a definite function in salvation history.[63]
He admits that "implicitly these titles raise also the
question concerning the relationship between God and
the person and origin of Christ," but he adds that even
here "the problem is not really 'a problem of natures.' "[64]
Moreover, and here Cullmann is opposing Bultmann, he
stresses that the concept of Jesus provided in the New
Testament was not exclusively determined by the meaning which the terms "Christ," "Lord," "Son of Man,"
"Servant of Yahweh," and so forth possessed in Judaism
and in pagan religions current at the time the New Testa-

was formed. He insists that we must be ready to admit "the possibility — even the probability — that in his teaching and life Jesus accomplished something new from which the first Christians had to proceed in their attempt to explain his person and work."[65]

Cullmann then begins a minute investigation of the meaning that the titles attributed to Jesus within the New Testament possessed and how they disclose to us Jesus' identity. The titles investigated are those of prophet, suffering servant, high priest, Messiah, son of man, Lord, savior, the Word, Son of God, and God. Toward the conclusion of his study, Cullmann observes:

> Our investigation of the Christological utilization of Kyrios, Logos and 'Son of God' has already shown that on the basis of the Christological views connected with these titles the New Testament *could* designate Jesus as 'God'. This is true for each title in a particular sense: the Kyrios is the present divine ruler . . . the Logos is the eternal revealer, who communicates himself since the very beginning; the Son of God is the one who wills and works in complete oneness with the Father.[66]

Consequently if we were to ask Cullmann whether or not the New Testament taught that Jesus was God, he would most certainly reply, "Yes." However he is anxious to distinguish between the functional Christology that he discerns at work in the New Testament and the ontological or metaphysical Christology that was at the center of the debates in later Christianity over the "natures" in Christ and over the kind of unity between the divine and the human natures in the person of Jesus. He prefers to consider Jesus' divinity exclusively from the perspective of redemptive or salvation history, particularly in considering the "preexistence" of Jesus. Cullmann views the whole course of redemptive history, as we have noted previously, as a line or movement or path whose midpoint is Christ. Every saving event that occurred prior to the life of Jesus pointed, representatively at least, toward him; every redemptive act that takes place in the Christian epoch is done in and through him.[67]

What does this mean as far as the preexistence of Christ is concerned? For Cullmann "the one upon whom all power was conferred, to whom all the Old Testament passages which speak of God could be applied, must have been at work already before his earthly life." And, he continues, "if this life" really is "the decisive revelation of God's redemptive will, then the redemptive line must also extend in the direction of past history to his pre-existence."[68] For Cullmann the recognition that Jesus is the midpoint of redemptive history, "the decisive, saving revelation of God," demands his preexistence, because "the Logos, who afterwards became flesh, is the bearer of all God's saving communication, even at the beginning; everything has been made through him."[69]

Cullmann also links the preexistence of Jesus to the notion that the self-communication or self-revelation of God is the glue, as it were, of redemptive history, for it is God's self-communication that binds together the various phases of that history. From the perspective of God's self-communication, we can say that "Jesus Christ *is* God in his self-revelation,"[70] inasmuch as it is in the life of Jesus of Nazareth that God's revelation of himself becomes tangible, perceptible. "If," Cullmann notes, "this human life, Jesus' atoning death, those events which can be chronologically dated, present the revelation of God as his decisive action, then . . . all of God's revelation . . . must be related to this centre in Christ, to this earthly Jesus of Nazareth, the crucified and risen."[71]

Cullmann's image of Jesus differs, obviously, from that afforded in the writings of his contemporary, Rudolf Bultmann; and certainly it should be apparent that Cullmann's views are more "conservative" and in keeping with the traditional teaching of the Church regarding Christ than is the thought of Bultmann. This does not mean, however, that Cullmann is a naive literalist, for in formulating the teaching of the New Testament about Jesus, Cullmann has exercised a great deal of critical discrimination. He admits that many elements in the Gospels are later embellishments and that the Jesus presented to us in the Gospels is a Jesus viewed in the light of the resurrection faith of the early Church, so that the events in his life were reinterpreted on the basis of this faith. He admits that Jesus himself was extremely reluctant to apply the title "Messiah" or "Christ" to himself — although for reasons quite different from those that Bultmann assigned to Jesus' failure to claim this title. However — and here we see the major differences between Cullmann and Bultmann — Cullmann is convinced first of all that the biblical critic should not carry over into his exegesis his own philosophical presuppositions. He acknowledges that those "elements [of the New Testament] really associated with a bygone world-view or [really] an outmoded form of expression may and must be stripped away as an exterior garb."[72] However he is totally at odds with Bultmann when it comes to the role that a contemporary world view plays relative to our understanding of the meaning of the New Testament. He insists that "we must reject the false notion that our separation from the biblical witnesses has been caused by the progress of modern science, so that today we cannot believe in salvation history because our world-view has changed."[73] Faith today, he claims, is no more difficult than it was for men of New Testament times. This does not mean that faith is easy; it is always a "scandal" and a "foolishness," but the mere fact that our scientific picture of the world differs from that of the biblical writers is not, strictly speaking, relevant.

Above all, Cullmann differs from Bultmann in insisting that the elements deemed inauthentic in the biblical message by Bultmann are so regarded primarily because of his existentialist philosophy, and not because their inauthenticity is demanded either by a contemporary world view or by the biblical data themselves, even as reconstructed according to the clues provided by the form critical method.[74] Consequently it would seem that the basic divergences in the image of Jesus in the writings of Bultmann and Cullmann ultimately derive, not from a difference in biblical methodology but from a basic cleavage in the mental framework into which the biblical data are received.

3. Jesus and Speculative Theology

Some of the dominant themes of contemporary New Testament scholarship of importance for our understanding of Jesus were investigated in the previous chapter. There in particular we summarized the conflicting views of two representative biblical theologians, Rudolf Bultmann and Oscar Cullmann. This chapter will explore the thought of some outstanding contemporary theologians whose approach to the mystery of Christ, although deeply affected by current New Testament studies, is more "speculative" or "systematic" or "cultural" in character. Because of the intrinsic value and influence of their views on Jesus, we have decided to consider the christological thought of the following theologians: (1) Karl Barth, (2) Paul Tillich, (3) Dietrich Bonhoeffer, (4) Wolfhart Pannenberg, and (5) Karl Rahner. In a subsequent chapter attention will focus on some significant contributions by contemporary theologians who seek to answer the question "Who is Jesus?" within the framework of an evolutionary world view or of a world "in process."

Karl Barth

Universally recognized as one of the greatest Protestant theologians of the present century, Barth was born in Switzerland in 1886 and died in 1969 in Basel, where he had gone after being forced to leave a post at the University of Bonn because of his opposition to the Nazi regime. During his student days and early years in pastoral work, European Protestantism was characterized by a great optimism for the future, "faith" in human progress, and a somewhat romantic and "liberal" view of Jesus as the supreme ethical teacher of mankind and the advocate of the universal brotherhood of man under the fatherhood of God. Toward the end of the First World War, and motivated primarily by pastoral concern, the young Barth began a serious study of Paul's Epistle to the Romans, publishing his commentary in 1918 and again, in a radically revised version, in 1922. The publication of Barth's commentary on Romans, particularly the second edition, marks a turning point in twentieth-century theology, for in it Barth directed a scathing attack against the liberal Protestantism so prevalent in his day, claiming that its subjectivism and concern to accommodate the Gospel to the dominant philosophies of the time had utterly distorted the good news proclaimed by Jesus and had, indeed, confused man with God and had put man in the place of God. The basic theme of this early work can be summarized as, "Let God be God, and let man learn again how to be man instead of trying to be God." In probing the meaning of Paul's Epistle, Barth had discovered that what is important is not what man thinks about God but what God thinks about man, and what God has told us about himself.[1] And to perceive this truth, to accept it, has profound repercussions on our understanding of theology and of Christ.

In Barth's view theology does not arise from human speculation, but rather stems from God's initiative and revelation. The inexhaustible subject of theology is the "God of the Gospel," the God "who mercifully dedicates and delivers himself to the life of all men" but nonetheless "transcends not only the undertakings of all other men but also the enterprise . . . of theologians. He is," Barth continues, "the God who again and again discloses himself anew and must be discovered anew, the God over whom theology neither has nor receives sovereignty."[2] In short the God of Christian theology can never be caught in a box and neatly packaged, once and for all, to be handled and conveniently categorized by men. No! He is an unfathomable mystery, utterly transcendent to and different from the creatures dependent on him for their being. Yet at the same time, this "wholly other" God can and does show mercy. Barth writes:

> He exists neither *next* to man nor merely *above* him, but rather *with* him, by him, and, most important of all, *for* him. He is *man's* God not only as Lord but also as father, brother, friend; and this relationship implies neither a diminution nor in any way a denial, but instead, a confirmation of his divine essence itself.[3]

This God in other words is our Immanuel. He is God with us, and man can never come to a knowledge of this living God by his own unaided reason. Man's reason may, indeed, argue to an absolute or supreme being or first uncaused cause, but the "gods" discovered by rational arguments are, in Barth's eyes, idolatrous inventions of the human mind and *not* the God revealed in Jesus Christ. The one, true God can be known *only* through Jesus, only through the mediation of the one in whom God reveals himself to man and in whom man sees and knows God.[4]

In other words, for Barth, *theology is christology.* The whole Christian message means simply "Jesus Christ," and Barth conceives the task of the theologian to show, as precisely as possible, what this means and how the revealing Christ tells us who God is and who we are.[5]

Because of this notion of theology as radically christocentric and because he is utterly convinced that "in Jesus Christ God becomes and is man, the fellow-man of all men,"[6] there is an emphasis on the divinity of Jesus in Barth's theology that is quite striking, particularly so today when the majority of theologians are more concerned with exploring and stressing the true humanity of Christ. Jesus Christ is for Barth the God who goes into the "far country," and if we accept the witness of the New Testament, there can be absolutely no doubt that the man Jesus of Nazareth is "by nature God."[7] In stressing the true divinity of the man Jesus, Barth is exceptionally eloquent and moving. For instance, in one text he writes:

There is no discernible stratum of the New Testament in which — always supposing his genuine humanity — Jesus is in practice seen in any other way or . . . judged in any other way than as the One who is qualitatively different and stands in an indissoluble antithesis to His disciples and all other men, indeed, to the whole Cosmos. There is no discernible stratum that does not in some way witness that it was felt that there should be given to this man, not merely human confidence, but that trust, that respect, that obedience, that faith which can properly be offered only to God.[8]

Or again:

What these men saw and heard, what their hands touched, was the fulfilment of the covenant in the existence and appearance of the one human partner who was obedient to God. This fulfillment was the Lord who as a servant lived, suffered, and died in the place of the disobedient; the Lord

who uncovered but also covered their folly, taking upon himself
and taking away, their guilt, uniting them and reconciling
with their divine partner. In the death of this Lord they saw
the old contender *against* God overcome and vanquished,
and in the life of this Lord, another man come forward, the
new contender *for* God. In him they saw the hallowing of God's
name, the coming of his kingdom, the fulfilling of his will
on earth. In this event in time and space, in the "flesh,"
they were allowed to hear the Word of God in its glory, as
a pledge, warning, and consolation to all men.[9]

Consequently Barth has little patience with those who
distinguish between the Jesus of history and the Christ
of faith. Barth holds that this is a false dichotomy, a
pseudoproblem. He is willing to admit that the apostles
did not realize fully who Jesus was until after the resurrection, but he is adamant in his insistence that the Jesus
Christ proclaimed in the Gospels is at one and the same
time the Jesus of history and the Christ of faith. The so-
called Jesus of history and Christ of faith are, Barth holds,
"abstract images," whereas the one Jesus Christ "proclaimed concretely" by the apostles was the one "who
had encountered them as the one who he was, even when
they did not believe in him. Having their eyes opened by
his resurrection, they were able to tell who he was who
had made himself known to them *before* the resurrection."[10]

The startling, ever fresh and astonishing[11] message of
Christianity is its claim that "without reservation or sub-
traction God was truly and altogether in Christ . . . that
God for His part is God in His unity with this creature,
this man, in His human and creaturely nature — and this
without ceasing to be God."[12] Because this is *the* revelation of God, Barth has no difficulty in accepting the
definitions of the early christological councils regarding
the divinity of Jesus and the interrelationship between
the human and the divine in Jesus. He believes that these

definitions were "factually right and necessary," yet he thinks that these formulae have been used too frequently to construct abstract doctrines about the being of the God-Man and to serve polemical and apologetic aims, whereas their primary value is their function as guidelines "for an understanding of His existence and action."[13] In Barth's view it is wrong to divide the Church's teaching on Jesus into christology — where attention focusses on questions about the interrelationship between the divine and the human in Jesus — and soteriology — where concern centers on his mission and work. To accept this division, as many theologians do, is to run the danger of misconceiving the whole import of the incarnation and to objectify or "thingify" the living, saving Christ. For the heart, the center, the essence of the Gospel and of Christianity is the significance of Jesus as the *reconciling* Christ, and this means that both the person and the work of Jesus must be viewed as one, as a single, undivided act. Jesus' "being as God and man and God-man," writes Barth, "consists in the completed act of the reconciliation of man with God."[14]

Barth develops his teaching on the reconciling Christ within the framework of a theology of the covenant or pact that God freely made with men. Reconciliation is the divine, saving act restoring the fellowship God intended to have with man and that had been destroyed by man's sin. Consequently reconciliation is a work of God's fidelity to his word, and in Jesus God is faithful to himself as the God who is eternally "for us."[15] Jesus is not primarily and in himself the one who overcomes sin but the fulfillment in time of God's eternal Word. Jesus *is* God's eternal covenant, moreover, precisely as the one who brings men salvation in time. He is the preexistent Word or Logos, but he is from eternity the Word that will become flesh; that is, from eternity he is the preexistent

"God *for us,*" the God who is our fellow human, our brother.[16]

Barth brings out the significance of the reconciling Christ by examining the meaning that Jesus has as (1) the Lord as Servant, (2) the Servant as Lord, and (3) as true Witness. Consequently, in order to round out this sketch of Barth's theology of Jesus, we shall briefly examine some of the major ideas brought out by him in his consideration of Jesus' person and work under these three headings.

In considering Jesus Christ, the Lord as Servant, we are, Barth tells us, considering the mystery of Jesus as a movement wholly from above to below, from God to man. The mystery of Jesus' true Godhood is the mystery of his *becoming man while remaining God.* "In Jesus Christ," writes Barth,

> God becomes and is man, the fellow-man of all men . . . and therefore Thou . . . *the* human Thou, which as such is also directly the Thou of the one eternal God . . . . God Himself, in His deep mercy and His great power, has taken it upon Himself to exist also in human being and essence in His Son, and therefore to become and be a man, and therefore the incomparable Thou.[17]

Yet, in becoming man and in humbling himself by taking on the form of a servant, Jesus did not to cease to be what he is, that is, God's Son by nature – true God. "He went into a strange land, but even there, and especially there, He never became a stranger to Himself."[18]

The mystery of Jesus' divinity is also the mystery of his self-humiliation, for in the incarnation God not only became true man but also accepted completely the totality of the human condition, becoming subject to death and judgment. This is a mystery that is a scandal and a foolishness. If we think that it is impossible for God to remain God while being true man, then we are simply wrong. We learn who God is, Barth constantly asserts, from what he tells us about himself and from what he does. "If He has revealed Himself in Jesus Christ as the God who does this (that is, becomes man while remaining God), then it is not our business to be wiser than He is and to say that this is in contradiction with the divine essence."[19] The incarnation is the revelation of God's supreme freedom and incomparable love. God in Christ, "far from being against Himself, or at disunity with Himself," has disclosed the "freedom of His divine love, the love in which He is divinely free. He has therefore done and revealed that which corresponds to His divine nature." Nor, Barth adds, does God's immutability or unchangeability prevent him from doing this. God's immutability "must not be denied, but this possibility is included in His inalterable being."[20]

It is as Servant that Jesus is one with us; it is as Servant that he becomes the contender *for* God and renders to the Father the obedience that God demands from His covenanted people. And it is as Servant that Jesus brings about our reconciliation with the Father. Nevertheless, and Barth is at pains to emphasize this point, the reconciliation that Jesus brings is, as such, a *divine* act, an act of God. Jesus' atoning act is "a sovereign act of God . . . of God's grace . . . original, unilateral, glorious and truly divine."[21]

When we consider Jesus Christ, the Servant as Lord, we are looking at the mystery of Jesus as a movement wholly from below to above, from man to God. For this mystery of Jesus is simultaneously wholly a movement from above to below and from below to above. In and through the exaltation of Jesus, the obedient Servant, to sovereign Lord all men are raised to fellowship with God. In developing his reflections on Jesus' Lordship, Barth makes it clear that true knowledge of what and who man is comes only through knowing Jesus. Human nature must be understood in the light of the nature of Jesus. Adam, as Romans 5, 14 tells us, "prefigured the One to come." For Barth this means that Adam is *derived* man and that the true image of man is the image given us in the "one who was to come," that is, in Jesus.[22]

Jesus is "man totally and unreservedly as we are,"[23] and in Jesus God takes human being into unity with his own, uniting to himself the *humanum* of all men. Because God became man in Jesus, Jesus is the promise of a basic alteration and determination of what we all are simply as men.[24] In conjunction with this idea of a new creature, a new mankind in Jesus, Barth develops the notion that Jesus is the *whole Christ,* the head of his body that is the Church. This means that the human nature brought into unity with God himself in the God-man Jesus is implicity the human nature of all men. As Barth writes:

> In Him we do not all exist as men *(homines)*, but our humanity *(humanitas)* as such − for it is both His and ours − does exist in and with God Himself. And where this is known in faith by the awakening power of the Holy Spirit, there arises and is, not a second Jesus Christ, a second Head, but the second form of His one existence, His people as the second form of His body, the community of those who . . . finding their own humanity caught up in His, and therefore exalted as such into existence in and with God.[25]

Note that here Barth insists that the community of which Jesus is the head is not an extension or repetition of the incarnation. Rather it *is* the incarnation, but in a "second form." Jesus exists as the whole Christ.

Because the human nature of Jesus is united to or one with God himself, through Jesus all men are exalted to harmony with the divine will. "We may indeed say," observes Barth, "that the grace of the origin of Jesus Christ means the basic exaltation of His human *freedom* to its *truth*, i.e., to the obedience in whose exercise it is not superhuman but true human freedom."[26] Jesus was the perfectly obedient and, consequently, sinless man, and in and through him all men are called to the same obedience and sinlessness.

However, and this is extremely important, Barth insists that the exaltation of human nature in Jesus does *not* mean the divinization of human nature or of man. Man, he insists, does not become God but God becomes man! In itself and apart from God's act the humanity of Jesus is not even exalted. Apart from this act it does not even exist.[27] The human nature or essence of Jesus is, Barth holds, to be regarded as a created or creaturely medium for Jesus' divine action, and this action, precisely as divine, is an act of God Himself. As Barth himself expresses this thought:

> We insist that its function is that of an organ of the Son of Man who is also and primarily the Son of God. It is to Him and not to this organ, not to His human essence as such, that there is given "all power in heaven and in earth" (Mt 28:18). It does not possess, but it mediates and attests the divine power and authority. It bears and serves it . . . . It is not, therefore, itself a divinely powerful and authoritative essence in which Jesus Christ, very God and very man, the divine Subject existing and acting in the world, makes use of His divine power and authority. But it is empowered as the necessary creaturely medium for His action.[28]

What all this means is that for Barth the union of the divine and the human in Jesus must be considered in a dynamic, active sense, and that we must avoid at all costs the temptation to conceive Jesus' human nature and divine nature in a static manner. We must not consider these as "things" or "objects" or "states." Rather we must consider their active and actual unity. Jesus exists in the unity of the movement from above to below and from below to above; he exists in the dynamic movement of God humbling himself by his gracious love and of man exalted in the act of receiving that grace.[29] It is this active, dynamic character of the union between God and man, between servant and Lord, that is brought to the fore in Barth's development of the theme, Jesus Christ, the Servant as Lord.

In considering Jesus as the true witness, Barth seeks to show how the mystery of Jesus is not only a movement from above to below and from below to above but also a movement outward. The incarnation is not only a reconciling act but a revealing or revelatory act or word. Jesus is the true light that enlightens all mankind. Jesus' divine-human existence is not something abstract and objectifiable. It is the good news that is the Gospel. It is life and meaning, and it is these now, today. Jesus, Barth reminds us, is the Risen One, and "He lives as and because He is risen . . . . If there is any Christian and theological axiom, it is that Jesus Christ is risen, that He is truly risen."[30]

As risen Lord and revealing Word, Jesus "is the total and complete declaration of God concerning Himself and the men whom He addresses in His Word."[31] Nothing can supplant the role of Jesus as the revealing word, not even the Church. For although Jesus is present in the world today and active among men in the body of which he is the head, we must maintain, Barth declares, that Jesus remains the head. This means that he is not subject to the Church, that the Church does not possess him as an object given once and for all. Rather Jesus possesses the Church and the task of the Church is to be the faithful reflection of Jesus active within the world. But this is a task in which the Church has failed time and time again; thus the need for constant reformation within the Church, within the body of Christian believers, to bring them ever closer in their conformity to Jesus and to make their lives truly lives "in Christ."

These are the major themes elaborated by the great Swiss theologian in his efforts to seek an understanding of his faith in the mystery of Jesus. There is, as noted previously, a marked emphasis in his writings on the divinity of Jesus. In addition there is a tendency to an extreme "actualism" in his way of regarding the interrelation between the divine and the human in Jesus. He insists so strongly and repeatedly on the divine activity in Jesus that at times it seems as though there is no real place for the activity of Jesus' human nature. Yet Barth strenuously rejects any charge that his teaching is in any way docetist or in any way rejects the full, total humanity of Jesus. The union of God and man in Jesus is a mystery, Barth maintains, and he holds that it is absolutely imperative to maintain that reconciliation is God's act, not man's; thus the emphasis on the divine activity in and through the person Jesus.

Paul Tillich and Jesus as the Christ

Of all the theologians of the present century, Paul Tillich is perhaps the most philosophical in his approach. Born in Germany in 1886, he earned doctorates in both philosophy and theology, and for a period he was the colleague of the famous existentialist philosopher, Martin Heidegger, at the University of Marburg. In 1933, because of his opposition to Hilter, he emigrated to the United States, where he taught first at Union Theological Seminary, then at Harvard University, and finally at the University of Chicago until his death in 1965.

Deeply influenced by the existentialist currents in Europe and by the impact of depth psychology, Tillich became convinced that theology, if it is to be a genuinely "saving" theology, must address the concrete situation of man, that it must come to grips with his "real, throbbing problems of life and death."[32] Perceiving in addition that many themes in theology have a great kinship to the themes explored by existential thinkers and depth psychologists, he concluded that the theologian, in order to carry out his work, must employ philosophy as well as theology. As a result the "method of correlation" that he follows as a theologian combines existential analysis and theological reflection. The basic idea underlying this method is that man cannot and will not receive answers to questions that he has never really asked. While it is true that "God in his abysmal nature is in no way dependent on man," Tillich writes, God is, nonetheless, dependent on the way man receives God's self-manifestation.[33] Consequently, the method of correlation "explains the contents of the Christian faith through existential questions and theological answers in mutual interdependence."[34] This means that the theologian must first draw upon the insights that contemporary culture, in particular, existential philosophy and depth psychology, can provide in helping him to analyze the "human situation out of which the existential questions arise." For it is only then that the theologian can seek to demonstrate that "the symbols used in the Christian message are the answers to these questions."[35]

As a result of this way of looking at the theologian's work, Tillich leads us to his teaching on the Christ by first examining those facets of human existence that raise the searing, shattering questions of life and death to which Christ is the answer. Consequently, to appreciate what Tillich is trying to tell us in his reformulation of the teaching on Jesus, it is first necessary to see how he views the existential situation that clamors for the answer revealed in the Christ. Prior to plunging into Tillich's existential analysis, however, a short description of what he means by "symbol" will be of value, inasmuch as this term has a special and critically important meaning in all of his thought.

For Tillich myth and symbol are the language of religion, of man's encounter with the holy or with the *mysterium tremendum et fascinosum.* [36] In Tillich's view, all theological statements except one — and that is that "the being of God is being-itself"[37] — are symbolic. But precisely what is a "symbol"? Its meaning, Tillich says, can best be seen if we contrast "symbol" with "sign." Both symbol and sign are alike in that they point to a reality beyond themselves; but a sign, such as a traffic signal, is arbitrary and changeable at will and does not share in the reality to which it points, whereas a symbol, for example the king of a country, is not an arbitrarily imposed pointer and, more importantly, truly shares in the power, meaning, and reality of that toward which it points.[38] Because of this, the symbol "opens up levels of reality which otherwise are closed for us" and also "unlocks dimensions and elements of our soul which correspond to the dimensions and elements of reality."[39] In addition symbols are irreplaceable; they are born out of the "collective unconscious" of the human race and die only when they no longer respond to the "inner situation of the human group."[40] Since "symbol" has such a rich significance for him, it is no wonder that Tillich is at pains to make it clear that symbol is not a fiction or shadow reality but laden with power and meaning. Thus, he tells us, "one of the things I always forbid my students to say is 'only a symbol.' This bad phrase is rooted in the confusion of sign and symbol . . . . If God is the creative ground of everything that has being, everything insofar as it is must express something knowable about God."[41]

But why — to return to our main theme — does man's human condition cry out for Christ? Tillich's analysis of man's existential situation is extremely rich and pro-vocative, so that any attempt to sum it up in a few brief paragraphs is not only difficult but dangerous. Neverthe-less the main lines of his thought can be seen if we ex-amine what he understands by man's finitude and existential anxiety.

Man's finitude, of course, is not unique to him, for he shares it with every created being. Yet, of all creatures man alone is capable of self-awareness and of reflecting on what it means to say that he is *a* being. Man is driven by his very condition as man to ask the question of being, and the very fact that he asks this question shows that he is *a* being and not being-itself and thus shares in some way in nonbeing. How can man possibly share in non-being if he exists, if he is? This is possible, Tillich tells us, if we stop to think about the various meanings that the term "nonbeing" can have. It can mean, first of all, nothing whatsoever, pure nothingness. This kind of non-being is the nothing referred to when we speak of God's creation of man and the universe out of nothing, and this kind of nonbeing is in no way related to being. But there is another kind of nonbeing, a relative nothingness that *is* related in some way to every being that exists. This kind of nonbeing is related to being in the sense that it poses a threat or menace to being, that it resists being and has the power to negate or pervert being. Thus Tillich can write, "Being, limited by nonbeing, is finitude. Non-being appears as the 'not yet' and the 'no more' of being,"[42] or "Nonbeing is the negation of being within being it-self."[43] Death for instance is nonbeing in this sense, and it is this kind of nothingness, of a power menacing and inescapably confronting every created being that is a sign of its finitude.

The experience of finitude, moreover, gives rise to anxiety. And it is, Tillich notes, imperative to distinguish between existential anxiety and fear. Fear is psychological and as such is focussed on a specific object. Anxiety, on the other hand, is all pervasive; it shatters the human psyche and is, indeed, the "existential awareness of nonbeing."[44]

In addition to finitude and anxiety, an existential analysis of man's situation discloses his alienation and estrangement. To understand the force that Tillich assigns to estrangement it is necessary to say a few words about his understanding of existence and essence, for he sharply distinguishes between the two and the distinction involved is basic to his notion of estrangement. The distinction is lucidly made in the following passage:

> "Existence" is a most unrefined alternative to the word "being," because it omits the potentialities of existence which we usually call the essences of things. And they have being too; they are the *power of being* . . . . Here you have a clear differentiation between essence and existence, which are two types of being. And then there is, of course, that being which is beyond essence and existence and which . . . we call God – or, if you prefer, "being itself" or "ground of being." And this "being" does not merely exist and is not merely essential but transcends that differentiation which otherwise belongs to everything finite.[45]

Existence in brief is not a synonym for being, and in some ways it is *less than being.* It is, indeed, actual, but it is "less than it could be in the power of its essential nature."[46]

But what has all this to do with estrangement, the existential dimension of human existence that Tillich sees symbolized in the biblical story of the fall? Simply this, that existing man, from the very fact that he is an actual existent, "is estranged from the ground of his being, from other beings, from himself."[47] He realizes that his own personal existence is characterized by disruption, conflict, self-destruction, meaninglessness, and despair, and that this existential turmoil is rooted in the depths of his being. This existential estrangement is rooted in man's state as an actual existent being. Simply because he is this man in these circumstances here and now he cannot exhaust the power latent in the essence of man as such. Even in his freedom he finds that he turns away and separates himself from God, the ground of his being. He does this through self-elevation, as he makes himself his own God; through unbelief, as he denies his dependence upon God; and through his ceaseless self-seeking, as he uses his potentialities without considering their source or the will of the God who gave them.[48]

We can summarize all this by saying that human existence, as disclosed through existential analysis, shows us that man is a being scarred by anxiety. This anxiety points to his deepest need, a need for the "courage to be." And it likewise shows us that man is separated and alienated from God, the ground of his being. This separation, which in itself implies an original union,[49] demands to be healed. This leads man to seek for a source of courage; it drives him to seek "New Being." And it is this New Being, the Being who gives us the courage to be, who is revealed in Christian faith. As Tillich affirms: "Christianity is what it is through the affirmation that Jesus of Nazareth, who has been called 'the Christ,' is actually the Christ, namely he who brings the new state of things, the New Being."[50]

Right at the start it is important to note that Tillich, in presenting Christ as the New Being, insists that "the paradox of the Christian message is not that essential humanity includes the union of God and man," but rather "that in one personal life essential manhood has appeared under the conditions of existence without being conquered by them."[51] This is significant because it shows that Tillich will put his emphasis on the "essential manhood" disclosed in the Christ and that he will not be overly concerned with questions seeking to discover the interrelationship between the divine and the human in Jesus. Toward the close of this section on Tillich we will attempt to find out more precisely what he means by "essential manhood." At this point, however, we do want to show how he regarded the traditional theological efforts to penetrate the mystery of Jesus by focussing on the union of the divine and human natures in the one person of the incarnate Word. Tillich grants that traditionally the major issue in christology "was how to think the unity of a completely human with a completely divine nature."[52] Tillich believes that an inquiry conducted along these lines can only lead us astray because of the "basic inadequacy of the term 'nature.' When applied to man," Tillich writes, "it is ambiguous; when applied to God, it is wrong."[53] "Nature" as applied to man is ambiguous because it can mean either of two things: it can signify human nature in its essential, power-laden yet nonexistent state, or it can mean human nature in its actual existential and estranged state. "Nature" cannot properly be said of God because he is beyond essence or nature, and it is impossible to apply the term "divine nature" to Christ inasmuch as "the Christ is not beyond essence and existence."[54] From this it is apparent that Tillich is not ready to attribute true Godhood to the Christ, to Jesus*.

In fact we find that Tillich dislikes to use the name "Jesus" all by itself. In an exceptionally significant passage, he gives us the reasons why:

> The first step demanded of christological thought is an interpretation of the name "Jesus Christ," preferably in the light of the Caesarea Philippi story. One must clearly see that Jesus Christ is not an individual name, consisting of a second name, but that it is the combination of an individual name − the name of a certain man who lived in Nazareth − with the title "the Christ," expressing in the mythological tradition a special figure with a special function . . . the "anointed one" who has received an unction from God enabling him to establish the reign of God in Israel and in the world. Therefore, the name Jesus Christ must be understood as "Jesus who is called the Christ," or "Jesus who is the Christ," or "Jesus as the Christ" or "Jesus the Christ."[55]

What this indicates, and this will become clearer as we progress, is that Tillich sees a much greater significance in the title "Christ" than he does in the individual human being, Jesus of Nazareth.

Because of this we might suspect that Tillich is not overly concerned with the question of the identification of the "Jesus of history" with the "Christ of faith." He is, it is true, anxious to provide some kind of historical reality for the Christian message, for he frequently asserts that "Jesus as the Christ is both a historical fact and a subject of believing reception,"[56] and he stresses that "the name Jesus Christ combines an historical statement with a symbolic name."[57] Nevertheless it is equally obvious that Tillich is not particularly worried about the historicity of the man Jesus of Nazareth. This is very strikingly brought out in an exchange that Tillich once had with a student. The student had asked what would happen to Christian faith if it could be proved beyond a doubt that Jesus never existed. In answering this question Tillich was completely unperturbed, declaring:

> Oh, then, he had some other name! That wouldn't matter.

> I want to say that if we were able to read the original police
> registers of Nazareth and found that there was neither a
> couple named Mary and Joseph nor a man named Jesus, then
> we should go to some other city. The personal reality be-
> hind the gospel story is convincing . . . . And without this
> personal reality Christianity would not have existed for more
> than a year.[58]

Tillich, even in this passage, is anxious to save some
factual, historical basis for the Christian faith, and he
is ready to admit that "if the factual element in the Christian
event were denied, the foundation of Christianity would
be denied."[59] Still this passage does indicate that Tillich himself is more anxious to drive home the significance of Jesus as the Christ as the symbolic personifica-
tion of "New Being" and "essential manhood" than he
is to elicit commitment to a specific human being.

In addition Tillich is convinced that the traditional
way of describing the event of Jesus as the Christ in
terms of an *incarnation* can be misleading. He holds that
the term "incarnation" is adequate "in paganism,"[60]
but that it is fraught with danger precisely because it can
give us a supranaturalistic, superstitious, and magical
picture of what transpired in Christ. He holds that the
statement "God has become man" is not paradoxical but
"nonsensical." And it is nonsensical because

> it is a combination of words which makes sense only if it .
> is not meant to mean what the words say. The word "God"
> points to ultimate reality, and even the most consistent Scot-
> ists had to admit that the only thing God cannot do is to
> cease to be God. But that is just what the assertion that
> "God has become man" means.[61]

It is, I believe, instructive to compare the position that
Tillich takes here with the vigorous affirmation of Karl

Barth, discussed previously, that this is precisely what the statement actually does mean, although Barth, of course, insists that the truly astonishing fact of the incarnation is that God, while becoming true man, remains true God.[62]

If the incarnation is an inadequate and misleading way of speaking about the Christ event, and if the doctrine of the two natures in the one person is likewise inappropriate, then how should the mystery of the Christ be expressed? Tillich argues that the traditional teaching should be discarded and replaced by

> the assertion that in Jesus as the Christ the eternal unity of God and man has become historical reality. In his being, the New Being is real, and the New Being is the re-established unity between God and man. We replace the inadequate concept "divine nature" by the concepts "eternal God-man-unity" or "essential God-manhood."[63]

The key, I believe, to understanding what Tillich means lies in the term "essential God-manhood." In an essay explicitly intended to reinterpret the doctrine of the incarnation, Tillich declared that the phrase "essential God-manhood" simply "indicates that divine self-objectification and essential manhood belong together, because man is essentially the divine image."[64] If this description of what the phrase means does not at first glance appear too helpful, we should recall Tillich's distinction between essence and existence or between essential and existential being, and connect this distinction with Tillich's teaching that God in himself is being itself and that he transcends both essence and existence. As the reality "beyond essence and existence" and as the "power of being," God is *not* an object, a thing. Rather he is the abyss whence beings, objects, and things spring. And prior to their "objectification" as existents, they are objectified as essences, as the power-laden potentialities for existence. In fact, as we have seen, actual existence is in some ways a diminution of the being present to essential being and in man leads to anxiety and estrangement. And this is precisely where Jesus as the Christ comes in. In the man Jesus, whom faith accepts as the Christ, essential God-manhood — that is, the essential being of man that is the first objectification of the God who lies utterly beyond essence itself — appears in history, in actual existence. Essential God-manhood means that "there is one man in whom God found his image undistorted, and who stands for all mankind — the one, who for this reason, is called the Son or the Christ."[65]

And Jesus as the Christ is the New Being who brings to all men the courage to be. His existence marks the end of the time when man's essential being or his original unity with God stands over against his actual existence, commanding and judging it.[66] The New Being revealed in the Christ brings to all men the hope that the existential anxiety and estrangement scarring their souls can be healed and that they can be restored to unity with God. And because he is this New Being, Jesus as the Christ brings salvation to all men, for salvation is a healing, a "reuniting that which is estranged . . . overcoming the split between God and man, man and his world, man and himself."[67]

This in brief is the christology set forth in Tillich's writings. It must be judged a heroic, creative, and powerful attempt to reformulate in an exceptionally radical way the traditional teaching of the Christian community about Jesus. It was undertaken by a theologian with a brilliant philosophical mind, and it was undertaken with the conviction, on Tillich's part, that the conventional manner of explaining the mystery of the incarnation was no longer viable, and that the traditional doctrines of the incarnation and of the two natures ran the risk of making the Christian message a folk myth and superstitious idolatry.

Dietrich Bonhoeffer

On April 9, 1945, Dietrich Bonhoeffer was executed by the Nazis, a martyr to Christian values. Although he was in the United States in 1939 and was urged by his friends to stay here and teach, he refused to take this way out of the agonizing dilemma that Hitler's program of total war and genocide forced upon the Christian conscience. In a statement that gives us an insight into his character, Bonhoeffer rejected the offer to remain in America, declaring, "I shall have no right to participate in the reconstruction of Christian life in Germany after the war if I do not share the trials of this time with my people."[68]

This courageous Christian, born in 1906, studied theology and developed his vision of Christianity during a critical time in modern German history. Not only were the Christians of his day faced with the life-and-death questions raised by Hitler and his followers, they were also living during a period when the liberal Protestantism that reigned in German theological circles during the early part of the century was being challenged decisively by Karl Barth, who, as we have seen, was struggling to make theology *listen to* God rather than *talk about* him. At this time also Rudolf Bultmann was seeking to make the biblical message relevant to contemporary man by offering an existential interpretation of what he considered the culturally conditioned myths of the Gospel narratives. All these factors deeply influenced the development of Bonhoeffer's thought, particularly with respect to the way in which he tried to understand Christ and to make his presence felt in the world today.

Today Bonhoeffer is known chiefly as a forerunner of what has become known as "radical theology," for it was

he who coined the phrases that have become the slogans
of the exponents of various "death of God" theologies,
calling Christ the "man for others" and addressing himself to the meaning of Christianity "in a world come of
age." Because of this some may mistakenly conclude
that Bonhoeffer was purely and simply a revolutionary
figure in theology, ready to throw out archaic teachings
just because they are old and questing exclusively for
"relevance" and "contemporaneity." To think of Bonhoeffer in this way is to err grievously, because he was
an exceptionally serious theologian with a burning, consuming faith in the risen and present Lord.

Although we do have, in the form of reconstructed students' notes, one book by Bonhoeffer explicitly concerned with christology *(Christ the Center),* it is somewhat
difficult to give a synoptic view of his theology of Christ
because so many of his ideas were never fully developed,
are dispersed in many different writings, and are available to us only in fragmentary form. Nevertheless it is
possible to grasp the key elements of his image of Jesus,
and a clue is provided by a passage in one of his early
essays called "Man in Contemporary Philosophy and Theology" (1930). There he declared:

> Christ exists among us as community, as church in the hid-
> denness of history. The church is the hidden Christ among
> us. Now therefore man is never alone, but he exists only
> through the community which brings him Christ, which in-
> corporates him in itself, places him into its life. Man in
> Christ is man in community; where he [Christ] exists is com-
> munity . . . . Therefore man can no longer understand him-
> self from himself but only from Christ.[69]

This passage, taken from one of Bonhoeffer's earliest
writings, includes the basic themes of his entire theology:
Christ, the community, and the Christian form one organ-

ic whole, since "man in Christ is man in community."
As we shall see, these themes are deeply interwoven in
Bonhoeffer's image of Jesus. Although our attention will
primarily focus on those elements of his thought that take
up in a more specific way the issues traditionally discussed under the heading of "christology," we will find
that to grasp in a meaningful way his vision of Christ
some consideration of his views on human community and
on man himself is absolutely indispensable if we are to
understand his contribution to our understanding of the
mystery of Christ.

We can note, first of all, that Bonhoeffer is very similar to
Barth, whom he profoundly respected despite deep differences, in his attitude both toward the absolute centrality of Jesus for our knowledge of God and toward the
question of the "Jesus of history." Like Barth, Bonhoeffer was convinced that the only way man could come to
a true knowledge of God was through knowledge of Jesus.
This is vividly brought out by Bonhoeffer's distinction
between unredeemed man, the man who had in Adam thirsted
for a "knowledge of good and evil" and a lust to become
"like God," and the man redeemed by Christ, who through
him bears the "image of God" intended in creation. Unredeemed man can know *about* God, but only the man redeemed in Christ can truly know God. As Bonhoeffer expresses it:

> He has the knowledge of God, yet no longer as the man who
> has become like God, but as the man who bears the image
> of God. All he knows now is "Jesus Christ; and him cruci-
> fied" (1 Cor. 2.2) and in Him he knows all . . . . He knows
> God as the ending of all disunion, all judgement and all
> condemnation, as the One who loves and as the One who
> lives. [70]

Also like Barth, Bonhoeffer regards the question of the

relationship between the "Jesus of history" and the "Christ of faith" as a pseudoproblem. He concedes that historical science cannot prove or demonstrate faith, and asks where faith is to receive its grounds for knowledge when history is uncertain. In answering this question, Bonhoeffer shows how deeply interwoven are Jesus and the church in his thought, for he writes: "There is only the witness of the Risen One to himself, through which the church bears witness to him as the Historical One. By the miracle of his presence in the church he bears witness to himself here and now as the one who was historical then." [71] In brief we believe that the Jesus of history is the Christ of faith because the "Risen One himself creates belief and so points the way to himself as the Historical One." [72]

Traditionally Christian theology concerning Christ focussed on the relationship of the divine and human natures in Jesus in the unity of the one divine person. Bonhoeffer believed that this traditional way of approaching the mystery was valid to an extent, but chiefly in a negative way. What the formulas of the early Church Councils — in particular the Council of Chalcedon — did was to tell believers that faith in the reality of Jesus as God and man forbade them from "taking the divinity and humanity in Jesus Christ side by side or together or as a relationship of objectifiable entities." [73] By this he means that an understanding of the mystery of Jesus can never be attained if we think of the divine and the human in Jesus as two separate and inert substances somehow joined into one. In fact, Bonhoeffer insists, believers should not approach the mystery of Jesus with the question, "*How* could Jesus be both God and man?" for this question is incapable of being answered and in addition "is tantamount to going behind Christ's claim and providing an independent vindication of it." [74] The question for the believer is, "*Who* is this God-man, Jesus Christ?" Although we can never plumb the depths of who Jesus was, this is the right question; and it is a question that can only be asked by one who is already a believer, by one who is already "in Christ" as a member of the Christian community. In asking it we already know the answer in part, for faith tells us that Jesus is God "for us," that he is God become man. But this is for the Christian the right question to ask, and its answer must be sought in the context of belief in the incomprehensible mercy of God to us in Christ.[75]

Who then is Jesus? Bonhoeffer insists that Jesus is not God's Son by adoption, but that he is the true Son of the living God. In addition, he is not a God "clothed in human characteristics," a God "dressed up like a man." No. "He is the God who has become man as we have become man. He lacks nothing that is man's . . . . Of him alone is it really true to say that nothing human remained alien to him. Of this man we say, 'This is God for us.' "[76]

For Bonhoeffer faith in Jesus means that we see the saving God in a man who was as truly human as ourselves, and we must, in considering his Godhead, "above all speak of his weakness."[77] Jesus truly enters the world of sin and death, the world of Adam, the world under a curse, and goes incognito as an exile among exiles, as a sinner among sinners. By this Bonhoeffer does not mean that Jesus was himself a sinner. Yet there is a mystery here; for, as Paul tells us, he was "made sin" for our sakes. He truly became flesh, the biblical word for man unredeemed by God, and as a man just like us, he "is tempted on all sides as we are, indeed far more dangerously than we are." He was not, Bonhoeffer says, "the perfectly good man," for he did things that outwardly looked like sin, becoming angry, harsh to his mother, breaking the law of his people. He did, in fact, enter "man's sinful existence past recognition."[78] But — and here in

Bonhoeffer's eyes is the crucial difference — "everything depends on the fact that it is *he* who took the flesh
with its liability to temptation and self-will." And in the
light of this "he" we can dare make the most scandalous
statements about the humiliated God-man. The great mystery of our faith in Jesus is that he, precisely "as the
one who bears our sin . . . is sinless, holy, eternal, the
Lord, the Son of the Father."[79] And it is this humiliated
human being, it is this man who suffered crucifixion as
a common criminal who is, in and through the church,
"present to us only as the Risen and Exalted One," for
we "know that he is the God-man incognito only through
the resurrection and the exaltation."[80]

For Bonhoeffer the conviction that the cruelly humiliated
Jesus is indeed the Risen Christ and Lord of all that is,
lies at the very heart of the Christian faith. And this faith,
to bring in other elements of his theology, is possible
only because that crucified and risen Lord is, here and
now, present to us in community, in brotherhood. Christ,
Bonhoeffer declares, can be conceived of only "existentially, viz. in community. Christ is not a Christ in himself and additionally still in the community. He who alone
is the Christ is the one who is present in the community,"
and he is present in the community *"pro me"* — for me.[81]
In other words christology involves ecclesiology; Christ
and church are inseparable. "Christ," he tells us, "is
really present only in the church."[82] And Christ is present
to us in the church as the one who heals, as the one who
restores the bond between God and man broken by Adam.
In Jesus God has given "himself an I, opening the heart
of God," and reconciling men to himself.[83]

Jesus' vicarious suffering brings about reconciliation
with God and is the "life principle of the new mankind."[84]
In Jesus God reveals to us that he is not free *of* man but
for man, and Jesus is the pledge and promise of God's

availability. He tells us that God is " 'haveable,' grasp-able in his Word within the Church."[85] The church, through which the Risen Christ is present to us here and now, is "a communion created by Christ and founded upon him, one in which Christ reveals himself as the second man, the new man, or rather, the new humanity itself."[86] In the church, moreover, Christ exists as a "living address" to all men, summoning them to response. As idea, or purely in itself, the Word can, Bonhoeffer says, "remain by it-self." But incarnate in Jesus, the Word becomes "an ad-dress," and an address can only be between persons, leading to an answer.[87] And because Jesus is a living word demanding response, the grace that the church me-diates to man cannot be "cheap grace," or "grace with-out price and without cost," a kind of supernatural com-modity purchasable on easy terms.[88] No, the grace that Jesus brings is a "costly grace," the grace of true dis-cipleship. "When Christ calls a man he bids come and die."[89] Christ's grace requires us to have the courage to "love the enemies of truth," to "face our enemies un-armed and defenceless, preferring to incur injustice rather than to do wrong." The way of Christ, Bonhoeffer con-tinues, "is an unutterably hard way . . . indeed an im-possible way."[90] But this is the way that Jesus summons us to go, and indeed he is himself this way.

For Bonhoeffer — and here he is taking a position quite at odds with the tradition in Protestant thought — the entire natural world becomes of importance in the light of the humiliated one whom we in faith recognize as the Exalted One. "The concept of the natural," he writes, "must be recovered on the basis of the gospel."[91] All of nature, and not men only, is redeemed in Christ, because Christ is lord not only of the church but of the world. "Through the incarnation of Christ," Bonhoeffer tells us, "the natural life becomes the penultimate which is

77

directed towards the ultimate."[92] Christ for Bonhoeffer is not an object of religion, of piety, "but something quite different, really the Lord of the world."[93] And it is because Jesus is Lord of the world that Bonhoeffer is convinced that even in an age that is nonreligious, even in an age when the traditional props that in times past supported the Christian faith have disappeared, Jesus, church, and God still have meaning. He tells us that

> it is not with the beyond that we are concerned, but with this world, as created and preserved, reconciled and restored. What is above this world is, in the Gospel, intended to exist *for* this world; I mean that, not in the anthropocentric sense of liberal, mystic, pietistic, ethical theology, but in the biblical sense of the creation and of the incarnation, crucifixion and resurrection of Jesus Christ.[94]

Bonhoeffer was convinced that we had to be honest with ourselves and "recognize that we have to live in the world as if there were no God."[95] The stopgap God, the God who in times past was posited as an answer to the questions that had as yet not received satisfactory answers, was for Bonhoeffer an idol, a fabrication of the human mind. The living God, the God revealed to us in the humiliated and crucified Jesus, is not a stopgap God. Although this living God "allows himself to be edged out of the world and onto the cross," he paradoxically becomes the center of the entire universe by becoming, in Jesus, "weak and powerless in the world."[96] And this God

> must be recognized at the centre of life, not when we are at the end of our resources; it is his will to be recognized in life, not only when death comes; in health and vigour, and not only in suffering; in our activities, and not only in sin. The ground for this lies in the revelation of God in Jesus Christ. He is the *center of life*, and he certainly did not come to answer our unsolved problems.[97]

Jesus is at the center of life and through Jesus so is God, because he teaches us now in the community that we are how to live and who we are. "The experience that a transformation of all human life is given in the fact that 'Jesus is there only for others,'" Bonhoeffer writes, and he continues: "His 'being there for others' is the experience of transcendence. It is only this 'being there for others,' maintained till death, that is the ground of his omnipotence, omniscience, and omnipresence."[98] That Jesus is the center of our existence, the center of history, the Lord of the world is not demonstrable. It does not mean that "he is the centre of our personality, our thought and our feeling."[99] Bonhoeffer is insistent on this, for he never wants faith to rest on proofs afforded by depth psychology, historical research, or any human basis. When he says that Jesus is at the center of all human existence, he is not making a psychological statement but a statement about our "being a person before God."[100] The truth of this statement is known only because of our faith, only because the Risen One lives in our midst serving us and revealing himself only to the extent that we see him in our brothers, in our fellowmen, binding their wounds, healing the divisions that tear them apart, suffering their injustices to us. And we must do this in faith:

> Our brother's ways are not in our hands; we cannot hold together what is breaking; we cannot keep life in what is determined to die. But God binds elements together in the breaking, creates community in the separation, grants peace through judgment. He has put His Word in our mouth. He wants it to be spoken through us. If we hinder His Word, the blood of the sinning brother will be upon us. If we carry out His Word, God will save our brother through us.[101]

While Bonhoeffer in no way negates or minimizes the true divinity of Christ, we find in him an emphasis on the humanity of Jesus, on his weakness and humiliation that is quite striking and intimately associated with Bonhoeffer's insistence that the Exalted Christ lives in our midst in his church, in us. The Christ of Bonhoeffer is the Christ we encounter when we meet one another, when we break bread together as did the disciples on the road to Emmaus, when we return love for hate, when we bring about reconciliation.

Wolfhart Pannenberg

Currently professor of systematic theology at the University of Munich, Wolfhart Pannenberg is a relatively young man — the youngest, indeed, of all the theologians considered in this book, for he was born in 1928. Yet he has already become the central figure in a new school of German theologians called after him the "Pannenberg Circle." His views on the historical character of the resurrection have elicited wide and varied reactions,[102] and his extensive study of christology — *Jesus: God and Man* — is an extremely rich and provocative work, displaying a superb command of the immense literature and of previous efforts by theologians from the time of the apostolic fathers to the present to reach some understanding of the mystery of Jesus, exhibiting at the same time a creative and stimulating approach to the meaning of Jesus' divinity.

For Pannenberg, as for Barth and Bonhoeffer, we can know God "only as he has been revealed in and through Jesus."[103] We do not first know God and then come to a knowledge of Jesus, but only through Jesus do we realize that the "ground of reality about whom every man inquires, openly or concealed, consciously or unconsciously, is in its real essence identical with the God of Israel."[104] Consequently he sees the task of the Christian theologian to consist in establishing "the true understanding of Jesus' significance from his history, which can be described comprehensively by saying that in this man God is revealed," or more succinctly that "Jesus is the Christ of God."[105]

Because he regards Jesus as the historical revelation of the true God, it is important to see how Pannenberg understands revelation and the interrelationship between revelation and history. The problem of any theology of revelation, Pannenberg notes, is to show "whether an alleged deity is really God, i.e., powerful over all things." Ultimately the revelation of the true God can be seen "only in the totality of all events, insofar as what we mean by the word 'God' is the power that is powerful over everything that has being."[106]

Because this is the problem in any theology of revelation, the unique character of the God of Israel whom Jesus worshiped as his Father takes on special significance. For, observes Pannenberg, "it is explicitly stated in some Israelite texts that Yahweh will *prove* his divinity, for Israel and for all other people, through *events* which will show that the God of Israel is powerful over all things."[107] Consequently the revelation of this God must be understood to be first of all a "self-revelation" in the sense that the God of Israel establishes or confirms who he is through his actions in history. History thus becomes the means whereby we are to experience God's self-revelation or self-confirmation. Historical events are not, to be sure, direct revelations of God simply because they are not identical with God himself; yet they are revelatory experiences in an indirect way because from them we can infer that God truly exists and that he does what God is supposed to do, that is, exerts power over all that is.[108]

In addition Pannenberg insists that revelation does not take place at the beginning of history but at its end. And this is where the unique importance and significance of Jesus is to be found. Pannenberg admits that on his view of revelation the reality of the God of Israel can be seen clearly "only in the totality of all events." Consequently since the course of history is still unfinished, "the divinity of the God of Israel is, strictly speaking, not yet revealed but is still hidden." However, he adds, single events can in a sense anticipate the whole of history and "to this extent anticipatory revelations of the power over everything are thinkable . . . . The final, although still anticipatory, revelation of God is in Jesus Christ."[109]

Jesus for Pannenberg is the anticipatory revelation of God because Jesus is the *eschaton,* that is, the end of human history. Jesus is the end of human and indeed of world history, not in the sense that all events tend toward him by their own intrinsic nature, but "he is their consummation in the sense of something contingent but ultimate from which everything happening before . . . is illuminated and receives its true significance and thus its essence."[110] Why is this the case, and how is this to be shown?

The Christ event is the revelation of God because Jesus proclaimed that in him the reign or kingdom of God had definitively come into being and that the end-time of history was at hand. Pannenberg himself believes — and here he follows the lead of a large number of contemporary biblical scholars — that Jesus himself was of the opinion that the world would come to an end in the very near future, perhaps during his own lifetime. As events turned out, this was an erroneous expectation. Nevertheless, Pannenberg insists, it is still true that "the end that stands before all men" has actually occurred in Jesus, because this end is death and resurrection. The resurrection, consequently, is for Pannenberg "the actual event of revelation" and is so because it establishes the divinity of Jesus and confirms God's self-revelation in Jesus."[111]

Everything, consequently, depends on the resurrection of Jesus as the confirmation that he is in truth the summation of history and the revealer of the one true God.[112]

Pannenberg is convinced that the resurrection of Jesus from the dead is a historical event, that it really happened. He likewise insists that the reality of the resurrection as a historical happening is not to be taken on faith; for if its guarantee is pure faith, then it loses its significance as a real event in human history.[113] This does not make faith superfluous, for although we can establish the reality of the resurrection as a historical event by the methods of historical research, the inference from this historical act to the truth that God has truly revealed himself in Jesus requires an act of faith. As Pannenberg sees it:

> One cannot really know of *God's revelation* in Jesus Christ without believing. But faith does not take the place of knowledge. On the contrary, it has its basis in an event which is a matter for knowing and which becomes known to us only by more or less adequate information. To be able to have Christian faith one must at least presuppose that the message about Jesus Christ is true. This includes primarily the affirmation . . . that he really rose from the dead.[114]

Consequently Pannenberg argues for the reality of the resurrection as a real historical event. He is well aware of the various discrepancies in the biblical narratives of the appearances of the risen Lord and in the accounts of the empty tomb. Indeed the whole of his study of Jesus shows that he accepts the position that the gospel narratives reflect the faith of the early Christian community and thus retell the story of Jesus in the light of their faith in him as the Risen Lord. In fact one of his major arguments in support of the historical reality of the resurrection is that the emergence of primitive Christianity simply cannot be understood unless it is seen in the light of the hope for a resurrection from the dead, a hope rooted in the fact that this resurrection had already occurred in Jesus.[115] He likewise argues that it would have been impossible to proclaim Jesus as the risen one in Jerusalem, as the disciples obviously did, if the tomb were not empty.[116] In short all the data available to historical research converge so that the assertion that Jesus really rose from the dead appears "as very probable, and that always means in historical inquiry that it is to be presupposed until contrary evidence appears."[117]

Not only is the resurrection a historical fact, it is also — and herein we find its theological significance — the confirmation of the God whom Jesus called Father as the true God, the One whose power extends to all that is, and at the same time it is the grounds for Jesus' unity with God and hence his true divinity. We shall first see how the resurrection establishes Jesus' divinity and then see how it confirms the reality of the God of Israel whom Christians, through Jesus, call upon as their Father.

Of the several steps that Pannenberg sees leading from the resurrection to the establishing of Jesus' true divinity, the most important lies in Pannenberg's observation that there is in the self-revelation of God an identity between Revealer and Revealed. This means that the one who reveals who God is must be one with God. Consequently since the resurrection shows that Jesus is the one who brings to man the final — although anticipatory — revelation of the reality of God, it follows that "Jesus belongs to the definition of God and thus to his divinity, to his essence."[118] By its own inner logic, Pannenberg insists, the resurrection compels us to affirm the preexistence of Jesus. It leads us to affirm that

> Jesus was always one with God, not just after a certain date in his life. And in view of God's eternity, the revelatory

84

character of Jesus' resurrection means that God was always one with Jesus, even before his earthly birth. Jesus is from all eternity the representative of God in the creation.[119]

Moreover — and here Pannenberg sees the beginnings of the Christian doctrine of the Trinity — the very fact that the history and person of Jesus of Nazareth are seen to belong to the essence of God makes it necessary for us to say that "the distinction that Jesus maintained between himself and the Father also belongs to the divinity of God."[120] When he attempts to spell out more specifically how Jesus and the Father are one, Pannenberg offers some suggestions that, despite their Hegelian overtones, are exceptionally illuminating and provocative. For instance, in speaking of Jesus' personal unity with the Father, Pannenberg writes:

Jesus is one with God through his dedication to the Father that is confirmed as a true dedication by the Father's acknowledgement of him through Jesus' resurrection. Such personal community is at the same time essential community. It is so first of all in the sense that it is the essence of the person itself to exist in dedication. Hegel said that it is 'the character of the person . . . to supersede its isolation, its separatedness' through dedication. 'In friendship and love I give up my abstract personality and win thereby concrete personality. The truth of personality is just this, to win it through this submerging, being submerged in the other.' To be submerged in the Thou means at the same time, however, participation in his being. Thus the divinity of Jesus as Son is mediated, established through his dedication to the Father. In the execution of this dedication, Jesus is the Son. Thus he shows himself identical with the correlate Son [the eternal Logos] already implied in the understanding of God as the Father, the Son whose characteristic it is not to exist on the basis of his own resources but wholly from the Father. The mutual dedication of Father and Son to one another, which constitutes the Trinitarian unity of God, also establishes thereby first of all the true divinity of the Son.[121]

Pannenberg's observations here are searching, and they do, I believe, help us to understand more fully what Paul meant when he spoke of Jesus' emptying himself of his divinity (see Philippians 2, 7) and to see why it was the second person of the Trinity, the Son, who became man and not the Father or the Spirit. Nonetheless Pannenberg's use of the monistic philosopher Hegel in describing the character of Jesus' personal union with God should serve to make us suspect that the Jesus presented in Pannenberg's theology may actually be quite different from the One in whom we put our faith. That this may be the case will, I believe, become a stronger suspicion after we see how Pannenberg speaks of Jesus as the Lord of creation, the summation of humanity, the "eschaton" or "end-event" revealing the God who has power over all that is.

Pannenberg insists that the resurrection establishes Jesus as the revealer of God's "eschatological will." That is, as was indicated previously, Jesus anticipates through his resurrection what lies in store for all mankind: death and resurrection. Because Jesus thus reveals God's will for the end or consummation of history, he is "the incarnation of eschatological reality," and from him we can anticipate how God's will for all men and, indeed, for the whole universe — which is meaningful only in relation to mankind[122] — will be achieved.[123] Here we must recall that Pannenberg insists that the reality of God is to be sought at the end and not at the beginning of history. Thus Jesus is significant because in him this end of history is truly anticipated and revealed. Jesus is Lord of the entire cosmos only because he sums up in his resurrection the process of the whole world toward unity. In fact Jesus is preexistent and, therefore, present at the creation only because the process of the universe toward unity — a process that will be completed only at the end of time — actually began with Jesus.[124] In brief Jesus is

Lord of all men and of the cosmos because he is established through the resurrection in a personal unity with God. And "because Jesus' unity with God is first decided by his resurrection, only through Jesus' resurrection is the creation of the world fulfilled."[125] We have already seen how Pannenberg conceived Jesus' personal unity with God. Now let us see how he links the unity of all creation with God to the achievement of Jesus. Pannenberg writes:

> Jesus in his dedication to the Father and to his mission for humanity is also in some sense exemplary for the structure of every individual event. Everything is what it is only in transition to something other than itself; nothing exists for itself. Every particularity possesses its truth in its limit, through which it is not only independent but is also taken up into a great whole. Through giving up its particularity, everything is mediated with the whole and, transcending its finitude, with God, who nevertheless wanted this particularity to exist within the whole of his creation . . . . Jesus' saying about losing and finding life (Mark 8:35) has universal ontological relevance.[126]

In this passage Pannenberg cites the Gospel according to Mark and not Hegel. And it is certainly true that the point he affirms is, in a very real sense, what is involved in becoming one with Jesus, for we are asked to die in order to live, and we are asked to give ourselves away in love, to "submerge" self in the other, in the neighbor in whom Jesus lives. Yet, the language of this passage is also very strongly Hegelian in its overtones and significance. For Hegel history was a dialectical process whereby the Absolute divested himself of himself only in order to return in a greater richness to himself. And this view of history seems to be deeply reflected in Pannenberg's vision of the significance of revelation and of the Christ event.

Finally, throughout his book on Christ, Pannenberg insists that the significance of Jesus lies in the fact that he is, through the resurrection, the "beginning of the end," the anticipatory realization of the consummation of the world in the unity of God. But what about God himself? Who is this being who is "the power that is powerful over everything that has being"?[127] For Pannenberg this God is present now only as the Power of the Future. "Since what we really are is not determined until the end, since all meaning and being are grounded in anticipation which is finally directed to that end, God is the all-determining power in the present *even though he is not now extant*."[128] In other words, creation is an act of God, as it is an act of Jesus, only *retroactively*, only in the perspective of what ultimately is at the end of time. God's being lies really, existentially, only in the future; it "was" at the creation and "is" now only because of the power of the future.

These aspects of Pannenberg's thought are noted chiefly because an awareness of them is crucial if his teaching on Jesus is to be understood. On first reading, his study of Jesus strikes one as exceptionally "orthodox," for he upholds the reality of the resurrection as a historical fact, argues for the "preexistence" of Jesus and for his personal unity with the Father, and provides the reader with a wealth of rich and provocative insights into the meaning and significance of Jesus. However the precise significance of his teaching on Jesus simply cannot be seen unless the Hegelian overtones noted previously and the radically different notion of God that he proposes — and which is not found in his book on Jesus — are taken into account. His reconstruction of christological doctrines then takes on a very different direction, one quite radical and novel in the history of Christian thought.

Karl Rahner

At present professor of dogmatic theology at the University of Munich, Karl Rahner (born 1904) is rapidly becoming recognized as the most important and profound Catholic theologian of the twentieth century. He brings to his work as a theologian a philosophical framework rooted in the tradition of Thomas Aquinas and rendered exceptionally creative by his own personal redirection and revitalization of this tradition through a fruitful and constructive confrontation with modern and contemporary thought. His probing inquiries have reached into almost every aspect of Christian life, and although he has not written a comprehensive study explicitly directed to the person and work of Jesus, the mystery of Christ is an underlying, pervading theme in all his writings.[129] Not only does he insist that the teaching on Jesus is the core of the Christian message, he takes care to show in detail how radically connected with Christ are all the truths of Christianity. The central position of the mystery of Jesus in the whole of Christian faith is strikingly set forth in the following passage:

> Christianity is the . . . historical event of God's self-communication. This means that the really fundamental Christian conception of the world (including spiritual persons) and of its relation to God is not to be found in the doctrine of creation, fundamentally important as this is. It is based on the history of salvation, which shows that the absolute, infinite, and holy God wills in the freedom of his love to communicate *himself* . . . to what is not divine . . . . Viewed in this light, Jesus Christ as the incarnate Logos of God is God's supreme self-communication. This takes place in the incarnation. For here God is so much the self-bestower that the "addressee" of God's self-communication is posited by God's absolute will to his effective, i.e., accepted self-communication.[130]

Rahner is convinced that the traditional teaching that Jesus is true man and true God must serve as the presupposition and starting point for theological inquiry precisely because this teaching expresses the "simple insight of the faith that this concrete individual [Jesus] who acts and encounters us is true God and true man, that these predicates do not mean the same, yet both are the reality of the one and the same being."[131] Consequently Rahner has a deep respect for the past teaching of the Church on the person and work of Jesus, and he sees the task of the theologian today to consist in expressing this tradition in such a way that it can be understood by contemporary man, with every trace of a mythological interpretation rigidly excluded.[132]

The problem, as Rahner sees it, is that the teaching about Jesus as true man and true God has, particularly in its popular understanding, been turned into a myth in which Jesus is regarded as God masquerading as man. "In the ordinary religious life of the Christian," he writes, "Christ finds a place only as God."[133] As a result, in his own searching investigations, he is anxious to avoid any danger of making Jesus appear as some kind of mythical divine man and to take as seriously as possible the Christian conviction that Jesus was truly a man, just as human as we are.

This concern is demonstrated most explicitly, as we shall see, in Rahner's discussion of the knowledge and self-consciousness of Jesus; nonetheless it is operative in his entire approach to the question of Christ. Rahner consequently sees the mystery of Jesus and the mystery of man as inseparable, with insights into the one shedding light on the other. Thus in setting forth his own creative reformulation of the Christian conviction that in Jesus God became man — or, in the language of the prologue to John's Gospel, that in Jesus the "Word became flesh"

— he makes a constant effort to show us how the incarnate Word helps us to understand who man is and how an understanding of man helps us to see who Jesus is.

From the time of Augustine, it has been customary in theology to take it for granted that anyone of the divine persons could have become man. This, Rahner maintains, is a questionable theological opinion, and it runs the risk of seriously misunderstanding the meaning of the incarnation. In his view it is very significant that the second person of the Trinity — the Son or Word, and he alone — became man. To show why, he develops a theology of symbolic reality. First of all he observes that all finite beings are in a very real sense "symbolic," because it is necessary for them to order to attain their full reality to "express" themselves, that is, to disclose or manifest themselves in different ways. Philosophers usually attribute this need of finite beings to their poverty of being, to their limitation, to the fact that they are mixtures of being and nonbeing, of unity and plurality. They are and yet they are not; they can act out the potentialities within themselves only bit by bit. Nevertheless, Rahner suggests, it is conceivable that this need of finite beings to express themselves symbolically reflects their relationship to God and reveals their character as "traces" or indicators of their creator. If this suggestion has validity, then we can say that the symbolic character of all finite reality is a "consequence of that divine plurality which does not imply imperfection and weakness, limitation of being, but the supreme fullness of unity."[134] And the meaning of a symbol or symbolic reality is to say that it "is the supreme, primal representation . . . in which one reality renders another present."[135]

Suppose that this is the right way to understand what is meant by symbolic reality. Then, Rahner urges, the traditional teaching of Christian theologians on the re-

lationship between Son and Father within the Trinity takes
on special significance. For in this tradition the Son is
described as the eternal "Word." As such he is the image
or expression of the Father within the triune God. But
this then means that the Word or Son is the "symbol"
of the Father, the inward symbol that remains distinct
from the Father whom he symbolizes while at the same
time being the perfect and total expression of the Father.
And here, perhaps, we have a clue to understanding why
the Word alone, and no other person of the Trinity, became man, for, writes Rahner "the immanent self-utterance
of God in his eternal fullness is the condition of the self-
utterance of God outside himself, and the latter continues
the former." [136] The importance of the latter part of this
sentence for understanding *who* man is should be obvious,
for the reality outside of God wherein he expresses himself fully is the created reality of Jesus' manhood. We
shall see the implications of this more fully later; for
the present we wish to show how seriously Rahner accepts the truth, constantly reaffirmed throughout the history of Christianity, that the Word became *flesh,* that God
became *man.*

If we are to take this affirmation seriously, Rahner
maintains, we must be careful to distinguish mystery from
myth. A myth — "God disguised as a man or God dressed
up as a man" — is a complete distortion of the Christian
faith, yet it is a constant peril. A mystery, on the other
hand, is not an imaginative construct but possesses genuine intelligibility, even if this intelligibility can never
be grasped exhaustively. [137] To prevent the Christian doctrine on the incarnation from becoming a myth we must
insist over and over again that Jesus, "in reality and
in all truth is man with all that this involves: a human
consciousness which is aware . . . of its own infinite
distance in relation to God; a spontaneous human interior

life and freedom."[138] It is so crucially important to realize this truth that, Rahner insists, we must be ready to say that there really does belong to Jesus' human nature "a personal (in the modern sense) centre of action of finite self-consciousness and created freedom."[139] The technical, precise meaning of the one divine "person" attributed to Jesus in the classical creeds, Rahner stresses, must not be taken to deny the reality of this "personal centre" of action in his human nature, otherwise we will in effect deny Jesus' true manhood, interpret the incarnation mythologically, and fall into the very errors that the early councils sought to eradicate by developing the terminology of one person in two natures to express the mystery of Christ. In the creeds of those councils the term "person" or "hypostasis" was used to designate the "bearer" of the divine and human reality or nature of "the concrete One who 'is' God and man,"[140] and to make it clear that the eternal Word is the center of unity of "God uttering himself and the created utterance in which and through which the utterance takes place."[141] The term was intended to show that Jesus is *one being,* and not an absurd union of two preexisting elements; it was definitely not meant to exclude a truly human center of operation, of freedom, or of what "person" means for men today.

Moreover, if it is really true that Jesus is a man just as we are, then this means that he had to grope for knowledge as we do, that he had to discover truths by trial and error, that he experienced moments of doubt and despair. This, indeed, is the image of Jesus that we find in the Gospels. Nonetheless it has been customary in Catholic theology to attribute to Jesus as man "a knowledge which embraces and exhausts all past, present, and future reality . . . . This theological tradition furthermore attributes to Jesus — from the very first moment of his human existence — the possession of a direct vision of God as it is experienced by the blessèd in heaven."[142] Statements of this kind seem almost mythological today, utterly contradictory to the real humanity and historical nature of the man Jesus. In fact,

> in view of the data provided by the historical sources regarding Christ's death-agony and feeling of being forsaken by God in his death on the Cross, can one seriously maintain — without applying an artificial layer-psychology — that Jesus enjoyed the beatitude of the blessed, thus making of him someone who no longer really and genuinely achieves his human existence as a *viator*?[143]

Rahner — and here his genius as a philosopher-theologian comes to the fore — argues that it is possible to reconcile the traditional Catholic attribution of an immediate vision of God to Jesus with the truly human character of Jesus' knowledge and self-consciousness. He agrees that human consciousness is a boundless, many-layered sphere that cannot easily be placed into neat categories. There is, for example, reflex consciousness of things that we know in an explicit, formal way. There is conceptual knowledge, expressed in clear propositions and in an objective manner. Yet there is also an "unreflected knowledge attached to the subjective pole of consciousness," a kind of knowledge illustrated by our own unreflective, nonobjectified awareness of ourselves. This latter form of knowledge, Rahner holds, is "a basic condition of the spiritual subject in which it is present to itself . . . . This basic awareness is not knowledge of an object, and normally one does not concern oneself with it."[144] Rahner holds that Jesus was aware of who he was — namely the incarnate Word — in this nonreflexive and deeply profound way from the very moment of his conception. The basis for this inner, nonreflexive, nonobjectifiable, and nonconceptual awareness was the hypostatic union, which "implies the self-communication of the absolute Being of God . . . to the human nature of Christ."[145] Nevertheless this basic internal awareness was not an explicit, formal, conceptual type of knowledge. Although it lay at the very root of Christ's human nature and was in itself his immediate "vision" of God, it would be a grave error to think that this required Jesus to have the "divine essence present before his mind's eye as an object, as if the divine essence were an object being looked at by an observer standing opposite it."[146]

Moreover — and here Rahner shows how profoundly the mystery of Jesus sheds light on the mystery of man — "the direct presence to God, considered as a basic condition of Christ's soul, must be thought of as *grounded in the substantial root of his created spiritual nature.*"[147] This means that, as Rahner puts it, "a direct presence to God belongs to the nature of a spiritual person, in the sense of an unsystematic attunement and an unreflected horizon which determines everything else and within which the whole spiritual life of this spirit is lived."[148] If this is true, then human nature can be conceived as "an active transcendence" or opening "toward the absolute being of God."[149] It means that man himself is an openness to God, a question addressed to God.[150] And if this is the case, then human nature, when it is posited by God as his very own reality — as it is in Jesus — simply reaches the point toward which it strives. The very meaning of human nature thus becomes an active possibility for being taken up by God and made into *his* reality.[151]

The meaning of man as disclosed in Jesus becomes even more apparent when we reflect on what we mean by saying that the eternal Word *became* man. The change or becoming involved cannot take place in the eternal Word, for as God this Word is immutable. Yet it remains true that this Word truly became man, and this means that the changing history of human reality is the history of the Word, that our time became the time of the eternal, that our death became the death of the immortal God. When we say that God became man we are saying that "he who is unchangeable in himself can *himself* become subject to change in *something else*."[152]

In the event of the incarnation, God creates what is not himself — namely a human being — and he retains this created human reality as his very own. But, Rahner notes, because "he truly wills to retain the other as his own, he constitutes it in its genuine reality."[153] Human nature is the same in us and in Jesus. The difference between us and Jesus is that in Jesus this nature, this "what," is God's self-expression, uttered inwardly in the Trinity through the Word, and now uttered outwardly in a reality that has become that Word's very own; whereas our nature, our "what," is not actually and substantially the concrete human nature possessed by the Word.[154] Yet the incarnation shows that our human nature is open to being possessed as God's own, and by the fact that God "pronounces as his reality precisely that which we are," he "constitutes and redeems our very being and history."[155] This means that we can truly define man, "within the framework of his supreme and darkest mystery, as that which ensues when God's self-utterance, his Word, is given out lovingly into the void of god-less nothing."[156]

Furthermore, because Jesus is truly man and shares completely in the human condition, the meaning of human death takes on a new light. Death, which Rahner sees as *the* act in which man as a free being disposes of himself in his entirety,[157] becomes redeemed and transfigured in Christ. For the death of Jesus, precisely because of its darkness and of its complete acceptance by him, brings it about that "what was once the manifestation of sin becomes, without its darkness being lifted, the manifestation of an assent to the will of the Father, which is a rejection of sin."[158]

Finally man can be said to be the "code-word" for God inasmuch as men exist ultimately because Jesus, Son of Man and Son of God, was to exist. This means that the God who reveals himself to us in Jesus is to be found "precisely where we are, and can only be found there."[159] Because of this, if any man resolutely accepts his own humanity, his own existence, we can say that he is really seeking Christ and is ready to accept him, whether he knows of him or not, or whether, having heard of Jesus, he rejected him because the Jesus put before him was a mythic "divine man" in whom he could not possibly believe.[160] Moreover, if we seriously acknowledge the truth of Jesus' saying that he is himself loved when we love our fellowmen, we will realize that anyone who is capable of bestowing absolute love or another human being radically and unconditionally "implicitly affirms Christ in faith and love," even if he has never heard of Jesus and his redeeming death-resurrection. This is so, Rahner teaches, because love of this kind is possible only because of Jesus. A human being, precisely because he is finite, limited, and untrustworthy, cannot be the basis for this kind of absolute love given unconditionally. Although it might be possible to see the basis of this unconditional love given to a fellow human being on an abstract and theoretical philosophy of absolute love, Rahner is convinced that existentially and practically such love is possible only in and through Jesus. "It requires," he says,

> a unity of love of God and of the neighbour in which love of the neighbour is love of God, even if only implicitly, and only thereby is fully absolute. By that very fact, however, it seeks the

God-man, i.e., him who as man can be loved with the absolute character of love for God, and seeks him not as an idea (for ideas cannot be loved) but as a reality.[161-]

The foregoing pages have attempted to present a rounded view of Rahner's rich christological inquiries. It is hoped that they will help readers see how creatively Rahner has reformulated the traditional teaching of Christianity on the mystery of Jesus and how he has sought to make this teaching credible for contemporary man by seeking to stress the aim or intent of this teaching while eliminating those historically and culturally conditioned aspects surrounding this aim that carry the danger of making the Christ of faith a mythic figure.

With Rahner our investigation of the image of Jesus set forth by some outstanding contemporary speculative or dogmatic theologians comes to an end. In the next chapter we shall focus attention on a representative group of contemporary theologians who could also be classified as speculative or dogmatic. However, inasmuch as they more explicitly bring to the fore in their consideration of the meaning of Jesus a world view conditioned by an evolutionary perspective, it seems better to discuss their position in a separate chapter.

4. Jesus in an Evolutionary World View

Ours is an age in which evolutionary ideas have taken deep root. Most educated people today believe that the human race is itself the result of an evolutionary process, and they believe their lives are immersed in a changing, evolving universe. They also believe that there is discernible within the universe a gradual movement forward and upward and that a study of the past history of this universe indicates that, at various periods of world history, something "new" has emerged, a new type of life, foreshadowed and prepared for by previous forms of life, but still radically different and previously unencountered. Because of this widespread attitude of contemporary man, it will be of value to consider the position of some contemporary theologians who have set out explicitly to restructure the Christian teaching about Jesus against the background of an evolutionary world view. We shall first take up the position set forth by a leading process theologian, Norman Pittenger. His views, as shall be seen, are presented in a conceptual perspective provided by the thought of Alfred North Whitehead and Charles Hartshorne, the two leading philosophers associated with process thought. Attention will then turn to the christology of two leading Dutch Catholic theologians, Ansfried Hulsbosch and Piet Schoonenberg, who find the proximate inspiration for their undertaking in the evolutionary view of the universe articulated by Teilhard de Chardin.

Process Thought and the Christ of Norman Pittenger

Process theology, as noted above, is the name given to that kind of theological inquiry that makes use of the ideas and conceptuality set forth by the Anglo-American philosopher Alfred North Whitehead (1861-1947) and by the American philosopher Charles Hartshorne (1896-   ). This mode of theological inquiry is characterized by its complete and serious acceptance of an evolutionary or "processive" view of the cosmos and by a conviction that God is not only the supreme cause of all reality but also "supreme affect." For these theologians God is "bipolar" rather than exclusively "absolute," "eternal," and "infinite." By calling God "supreme affect," process theologians seek to indicate that for them the major characteristic of God is not his aseity or quality of being the supreme and uncaused existent but rather his love. They develop Whitehead's teaching that "God includes both a 'primordial' (or eternal) aspect and a 'consequent' (or everlasting) aspect to show that he is both infinite and unchanging . . . and also related to and affected by all that goes on in his creation." God and world are reciprocally related, and this means that God's being is affected by what goes on in the universe that he created out of love. [1]

To see where Jesus fits into the scheme of things as conceived by process theology, a brief summary of the way in which process theologians view the entire universe may be of help, for this will give us a general backdrop against which their teaching about Jesus can be seen.

For process thought the universe is a unified whole consisting of constellations of "events" or "processes," and all of these concatenations or constellations of events are interrelated, interlocking, interpenetrating. Each event or process, moreover, is *not* a static thing or object; rather it is a dynamic movement, or becoming, in which the past is summed up, the present is accomplished, and the future is shaped. Each dynamic event brings to realization possibilities that are chosen among the vast range of possibilities available to it, and in so doing it qualifies and modifies its relationships to other events. Each event or occasion aims at satisfying the end proper to it, and by its decision to pursue this end, it cuts off possibilities not related to that end or that would be harmful to it — or by deciding not to pursue the end, it accepts possibilities likely to do it damage and keep it from the best realization open to it. And all the while each event or process or occasion is related to its environment, influenced by it and influencing it. Ultimately its environment includes the entire created cosmos, but proximately and immediately it includes those other events more directly related to the event in question. Moreover, precisely because each event is itself, because it is this rather than that, it has its own qualitative distinctness.[2] Finally because each event going to make up the entire cosmic constellation of events is unique, is distinct, and has its own novelty, the process continues on and on. And —

as these novelties, slight as they may seem to be, continue to occur, to pile up, to accumulate, they work towards even more striking novelties. Eventually something emerges which is most strikingly novel. Not by intrusion from outside, but by emergence from within, qualitative differences appear as the result of a vast series of quantitative differences.[3]

Because Jesus is truly a man, whatever else may be said about him, we can come to understand who he was only if we see at work in the most strikingly novel event called Jesus the same complex of factors that we find operative in the universe as a whole.

Jesus is, precisely as a true man, a process or becoming. Thus Pittenger believes it is nonsense to talk of Jesus as having a human nature in the sense of possessing a suit of clothes. "To talk about human nature as if it were a given fact, with all the 'thereness' and immutability of such a fact," Pittenger writes, "is to misrepresent the deliverance of human awareness and human experience, which insistently shows us to be dynamic creatures with a thrust or drive toward the realization of potentiality."[4] Rather Jesus' humanity must be seen, as must our own, as a becoming, as a "routing of occasions" in which his identity was gradually disclosed and in which his significance is to be perceived. For Pittenger this means that the event that was Jesus cannot be understood unless he is seen (1) in his relationship to the past from which he emerges and to which he belongs; (2) in his relationship to all those with whom he associated and who associated with him; and (3) in terms of his impact and influence on future history.[5]

If we look at Jesus from the viewpoint of his relationship to his past, we must first of all take note of his Jewishness. His ways of thinking and acting, his understanding of his own mission in life, his attitude toward people and their attitude toward him, were all shaped by the Judaism from which he emerged. Seen in this perspective Jesus, as pictured for us in the Gospels, appears as

> the true radical, who penetrated to the heart of the Jewish awareness of God and God's will as it had been worked out in history, who provided a fresh but not totally discontinuous

beginning in the understanding of man *vis-à-vis* that God, and who in doing this (both by what he said and by what he did, as well as by what he was) established a new intensity in the relationship between God and man.[6]

Jesus, consequently, seen from the vantage point of his Jewish past, set in an entirely new light the Jewish conviction that God was to be trusted, that he was true to his word, that he was a being consumed with a passionate love for the people whom he had called to be his own.

In his relationship to his contemporaries, Jesus displayed himself, Pittenger tells us, as the embodiment of an outgoing, active, and creative goodness. The impression of Jesus that strikes us on reading the Gospels is that of a man "who was recalled as being utterly loving in his relationship with others, however exalting and demanding may have been his words as he spoke of God's kingdom and its requirements."[7] In brief it can be said that the impression made by Jesus on his contemporaries was that of a man embodying love-in-action to such an extent that people were led to believe that in Jesus God had indeed come and visited his people.[8]

Finally, with respect to the impact that Jesus had on the course of history, we must confess that this has indeed been unparalleled. No matter what view we may have toward the resurrection accounts, Pittenger maintains, we must grant that even after his death Jesus found reception among the people with whom he had lived and for whom he had died. In fact his cross was seen by his followers as a sign of victory, as the symbol of the triumphant love of God at work in the world and in human life, and the stories of the resurrection certainly make us admit that Jesus' followers were convinced that Jesus had not only triumphed on Calvary but that "God had vindicated that triumphant act of self-giving by signs wrought

in history, such as the resurrection narratives.''[9] And
not only did Jesus make this impact on his immediate
followers, his presence is still felt in the world today,
so that the love embodied in his life and action "is con-
tinued, extended, conveyed, made available through that
historically grounded community which has come to be
called the Church, and which thus makes the event of
Christ and the achievement wrought in that event a present reality for men."[10]

Reflection on all these converging facts associated
with the activity of the man Jesus leads us to conclude
that Jesus was truly man, but that as man he was unique,
distinctive, "strikingly novel." But was the difference
between Jesus and other men one of kind or of degree?
In Pittenger's view this difference can only be regarded
as one of degree. Were it a difference in kind, it would be
difficult to see how the truth — traditionally upheld by
Christian faith — that Jesus was a real man, as fully human as we are,[11] could be given any meaning. Pittenger
therefore argues that Jesus differed from other men only
in the sense that he realized to an unsurpassed degree
the possibilities open to manhood. Thus for Pittenger Jesus
is to be seen as "the One in whom God actualized in a
living human personality the potential God-man relationship which is the divinely-intended truth about every
man."[12] By making Jesus differ from other men in degree
and not in kind, we safeguard the teaching that he is truly
man; for a "degree-christology" affirms that "Jesus is
indeed a man, in the usual or ordinary meaning in which
manhood may be predicated of each and every instance
of human existence."[13] Yet at the same time this degree-
christology

says that men are more or less men; that is, there is no
universalized manhood of an almost substantial sort, as an

essence which may be predicated univocally of all men and in which they share; there is only this man and that man, realizing their potentialities in various ways and with great or small differences between them — but with differences nonetheless. [14]

Thus Jesus as an individual, specific human person realized the potentialities of human existence in such a way that his associates could see in him an extraordinary human being but still a true man who in no way violated the ordinary conditions of manhood. [15]

Still Christian faith is convinced that in Jesus God himself is present and active. Indeed for a Christian it is in and through the person of Jesus that God's love is manifested in all its glory, and in the Christian tradition Jesus has been called true God as well as true man. Precisely how is this aspect of the Christian tradition to be interpreted today?

To answer this question, Pittenger notes, we ought first to have some understanding of how God acts in all human affairs. Then we may be in a position to determine more precisely how God may be said to have acted in the specific human and historical event we call Jesus Christ. The character of God's activity in all human affairs is described by Pittenger in terms proper to the notions of process thought. Hence in order that we may be able to see precisely how he views the activity of God, it will be helpful to cite the passage in detail, despite its length. It runs as follows:

God acts in human affairs through the fact of mutual prehension. The term "prehension" is a technical word to describe or denote the grasping-and-being-grasped which is the very nature of each occasion or event. Each of these prehends, and is prehended, by other occasions or events. But in and through these creaturely instances of mutual prehension, the divine Love operates . . . not against them,

not in spite of them, not by overriding them, but precisely
and genuinely in and through them. For God is not some
thing which is added to other things . . . . On the contrary,
as the chief causative element in all causes and the chief
affected element in all affects . . . God is present and God
is active in every cause and in every affect. But he is there,
not by dominating those causes and affects so that they lose
their integrity by losing their freedom; he is there as the
omnipresent lure, the omnipresent aim, the omnipresent a-
gency for effecting love in the world. Thus every occasion,
in its quality and in its own degree, is an incarnation of
the divine dynamic which we call by the name of God. [16]

God, in other words, is Love, ever at work in and through
the events that go to make up the universe. His aim, as
described in this passage, is to effect love, to do good
in the world. Because of this, Pittenger argues, we can view
God's creature, man, as an event or being in and through
whom God wills to incarnate his love, make it spread,
achieve its potential as a power of unity and reconciliation — and all this with respect for man's freedom and
personal initiative. Thus we can say that the very "ground
of our human existence" is "the capacity to live in love,
to become true men by becoming true lovers." [17] If this is
true, then we can say that in Jesus what was only potential
in human existence was made actual, for "what God pur-
poses and accomplishes in Jesus Christ is the fully adequate expression . . . of that intention. This is achieved,"
Pittenger continues, "through God's setting before the
historical existent Jesus his initial aim, through providing him with his vocational lure, and through the mutual
prehension which is found when God and man are in openness and interpenetration *one with the other in Love.*" [18]
Jesus' unity with God, therefore, consists in this unity
through love. Although many may argue that this kind of
unity is only a moral union of wills and not the substantial,

essential union demanded by "orthodoxy." Pittenger is convinced that this way of expressing the reality of Jesus' divinity is fully adequate. Moreover, he urges, in terms of process thought, a moral union of this kind is metaphysical, that is, equivalent to the unity traditionally affirmed in Christianity by means of the categories of person and nature. It is metaphysical, he says, once we realize that "love is not simply a matter of desirable human behaviour but is the very basis of the universe and the grounding reality in all creative advance."[19]

Such is the view of Jesus set forth in the thoughtful, stimulating work of Norman Pittenger. His ideas on the true humanity of Jesus, I believe, are exceptionally significant; his notion of Jesus as the man in whom God realized and made actual the "potential God-man relationship" intended for every man has affinities with Tillich's concept of Jesus as the person symbolizing the true meaning of essential manhood, yet it also bears similarities to Rahner's contention that the human nature of Jesus is the actualization of human reality as an openness to God. Yet it does seem difficult to see how the tradition of Christianity that Jesus is the eternal Word of the Father can be made meaningful within the context of Pittenger's theology of the Jesus event. As we shall soon see, "pre-existence" is equally a problem for a group of Dutch Catholic theologians who have attempted to reformulate the teaching of the Church on Jesus from the vantage point of an evolutionary world view taking its immediate inspiration from the views of Teilhard de Chardin.

The Vision of Teilhard de Chardin and the Christ of Ansfried Hulsbosch

Certainly one of the most influential, original, compelling, and creative thinkers of the twentieth century is Pierre Teilhard de Chardin (1881-1955). A paleontologist

and archeologist by profession, a Jesuit priest by voca-
tion, Teilhard sought to bring together the worlds of science
and religion and to heal the fissures that had seemingly
ruptured the unity that once had reigned between intelli-
gence and faith, the universe and God. In the pages to
follow, we will not be concerned primarily with Teilhard's
own views as such, because he never set out explicitly
to write a treatise on Jesus nor do his writings discuss
in any formal way the critical issues that have formed
the substance of this report: the interpretation that is
to be given to the Christian conviction that Jesus of Nazareth is true man and true God and the effort to see, in
some way or other, how the divine and the human are *one*
in the person of Christ. Nevertheless, because his vision
of man, the universe, God and Christ, forms the proximate
inspiration for a new approach to Jesus undertaken by
the Dutch Catholic theologian, Ansfried Hulsbosch, the
discussion of the latter's views will be more meaningful
if it is prefaced by a short resume of the major elements
in Teilhard's world view, with special attention to those
aspects of his thought directly pertinent to the positions
taken by Hulsbosch.

Teilhard begins by considering man's existential condition in which he finds himself trapped, as it were, inside
this "bubble of the cosmos," worried that the long history of the human race will ultimately come to naught.
Against this pessimistic view Teilhard sees the concept
of evolution as providing a meaningful and hopeful sign:
man has a special history and, if he carries out his re-
sponsibilities, a promising, remarkable future. The confidence generated by this evolutionary perspective, coupled
with Teilhard's Christian conviction that Christ, as Paul
tells us, is the origin, present center, and final goal of
the entire universe, led him to develop his own original
synthesis of evolutionary thought.

Convinced as a scientist that there is a continuity between the animal and human worlds and equally convinced as a Christian that there is, in Christ, an ultimate meaning and goal for the evolutionary process, Teilhard was led to suggest a "hyperphysics" and to argue that matter as such possesses a "within" as well as a "without." That is, he suggested that matter as such possesses a rudimentary form of "consciousness" that becomes developed in animals and becomes aware of itself in man. As a consequence — and here we find one of the major links between Teilhard's thought and the approach of the Dutch theologians — it is possible to argue that matter is a revelation of spirit or, perhaps better, that spirit manifests or discloses in and through matter.

This view is closely linked to his theory of "discontinuity through continuity," according to which something radically new emerges within the unfolding drama of evolution when a "critical threshold" is attained. By increasing "complexification" quantitative changes ultimately lead to qualitative differences and entirely new kinds of reality. This means that in the forward thrust of evolution matter becomes more and more complex and, corresponding to this complexity, more and more conscious, more and more revealing its "inner face" or "within." If we apply this hypothesis to man, we will be inclined to see him as a strict unity, as a material being that is capable, by reason of the state of "complexification" that it has attained, of performing "spiritual" activities, that is, activities utterly surpassing those capable of being done by material beings of less complexity.[20]

Although the evolutionary process has many blind alleys, many ill-fated gropings, on the whole it is a process with an upward ascent, an ascent marked by an ever-increasing development of personality. This process has led to the evolution of man as a person responsible for carrying the evolutionary process forward. Man, Teilhard believes, can become truly what he is intended to be only if there is an increase of love, for it is by a process of "amorization" that the human race becomes what it is meant to be: a commonwealth of persons united in selfless love. This process, Teilhard argues, is possible only if we postulate an absolute center of love in the cosmos, activating human beings to achieve this goal and assuring the eventual successful outcome of evolution as a whole. This center, Teilhard holds, is the risen Christ who is the personal center of the entire cosmos and the point of its final consummation − its Omega Point.[21]

This in brief is the vision of Teilhard de Chardin. It forms the immediate backdrop for an approach to the mystery of Christ set forth recently by the Dutch Augustinian theologian, Ansfried Hulsbosch. His approach was warmly seconded by two other Dutch theologians, the Jesuit Piet Schoonenberg and the Dominican Edward Schillebeeckx.[22] Schillebeeckx, however, explicitly disavowed the Teilhardian or evolutionary presuppositions behind Hulsbosch's efforts, and despite his approval of the general thrust of Hulbosch's arguments he did object strenuously to certain aspects of the position Hulsbosch outlined. Schoonenberg expressed general approval of Hulsbosch's efforts and proceeded to elaborate on the "preexistence" of Jesus, a topic that was inescapably forced upon Hulsbosch. Our attention in what follows will be given to the position set forth by Hulsbosch himself.

Hulsbosch is concerned above all to account for the *real unity* of Christ, yet he fears that the traditional teaching of the Church on the unity of two natures in the one person inescapably conjures up for contemporary man an image of a Christ "divided into layers." Thus he writes:

This history of Christology is at bottom a search for the unity of this person who became known as man and was confessed to be the Son of God. The Church in her confession has always held fast to the unity of these so diverse elements, but in speaking of "two natures" she has called forth a tension that has persisted until today and in fact is felt today more keenly than ever. What is inevitably conjured up is the image of a Christ divided into two layers.[23]

Because he feels so keenly the need for keeping uppermost in mind the concrete unity of Christ, Hulsbosch believes that an approach inspired by Teilhard's vision of evolutionary process has much to offer. In one passage Hulsbosch explicitly refers to the fact that Teilhard had made room for Christ in his new synthesis of evolution,[24] and he suggests that the real unity of Jesus can perhaps best be safeguarded if we approach the unity of the divine and the human in Jesus in the same way that Teilhard approached the unity of the material and the spiritual in man. Consequently in suggesting a "new approach to the person of Jesus," Hulsbosch takes Teilhard as his model.

Man himself is nowadays seen ever more in a unity of his being replacing a dualistic concept [of soul distinct from body]. Should not the same revision also take place in regard to the unity of Christ? I am convinced that it should. The early Fathers were already familiar with the idea that the unity of Christ shows a resemblance to man's own inner unity . . . it cannot be said that the divine and the human in Christ together form a third reality in the same way as soul and body were then seen to form a man. Today we can no longer accept the notion of man as juxtaposition of soul and body. He is an absolutely indivisible subject. Can this insight not give us precisely the clue to a better understanding of the unity of Christ?[25]

Just as Teilhard sought to explain the phenomenon of man by showing how man is *in continuity with the rest of the material universe,* so Hulsbosch seeks to understand the Christ-event by showing how Jesus is *in con-*

tinuity with the human race. We can push the analogy further: Teilhard saw man as something "new" in the universe because in him matter had reached a new "critical threshold," so that the potentialities implicit in matter, contained within the "within" of matter, were capable of realization. Likewise Hulsbosch sees Jesus as something radically "new" in the cosmos because in him mankind has reached a new "critical threshold" so that the possibilities open to man have become capable of realization. Thus Hulsbosch argues that the divinity of Jesus consists precisely in the perfection of his humanity.[26] That this is the direction of Hulsbosch's thought is clearly indicated by some key parallels that he makes. He argues, for example, that "the living being is not matter plus life but living matter. Man is not matter plus spirit but . . . animated matter capable of those activities that we call spiritual."[27] From this it would seem to follow that "Jesus is not man plus God but divinized man." Actually Hulsbosch does not himself employ this formula, but it is one suggested by the direction that his thought takes and is a point to which we shall return after seeing in more detail how he views the unity of the human and the divine in Jesus.

Jesus, Hulsbosch argues, is *known* as man and is *confessed* to be the Son of God. This means that Jesus is God by being man in a special way. The Son of God or the Word became man — that is the way in which theology has traditionally described the mystery of Jesus. But, Hulsbosch argues, this mystery has always been presented to us as connected with our salvation. Consequently, he continues, the

    actuation of that salvation can take place only in the sector of the human. This man is Son of God in that this man [Jesus] is in contact with God in a way that separates Him from ordinary men. But this can mean nothing other than a special way of being-man, since the whole actuality of the mystery lies precisely in the sector of the human. In reflecting on the mystery, it is doubtless convenient to set the two natures over against each other, but a divine nature juxtaposed beside the human gets us nowhere . . . . The divine nature of Jesus is relevant to the saving mystery only insofar as it alters and elevates the human nature. And whatever that is, it must be called a new mode of being man.[26]

Hulsbosch's point here is difficult to grasp. Yet it seems to be that the mystery of Jesus' unity as true man and true God cannot be appreciated if we think of his human and divine natures as externally juxtaposed realities — if we find the notions of "nature" at all relevant to the issue. The only reason for attributing a divine "nature" to Jesus seems in Hulsbosch's view to lie in the alteration or elevation that this nature can bring about *within* Jesus' human nature, making his way of being man a very special, unique way of being man.

Basically the issue comes down to this: Is Jesus Son of God because of what he is as man, or is he Son of God in virtue of something that is his *apart* from his being man? In answering this question, Hulsbosch first recalls his own — and Teilhard's — way of looking at living beings and at man. With respect to living things, Hulsbosch had argued that their "life" must not be sought in some separate element wholly other than the nonliving matter from which living beings emerge. Rather "life" is to be sought within possibilities latent in matter itself. In similar fashion he had argued that intellectual and spiritual processes in man in no way compelled one to affirm a spiritual or immaterial soul as a reality distinct from the body, but that the spirituality of the human person could be seen as the explicitation and actualization of possibilities implicit in living beings but capable of being made real only when a certain point of evolution had been reached. By viewing living beings and men in this way, Hulsbosch believes that "we have progressed toward a better view of the real unity of their being."[29] If this same way of looking at things is applied to Jesus, Hulsbosch continues, then we will see that to attribute his divinity to a divine nature distinct from his human nature would be just as alien to his truly unified being as a separate spiritual soul would be in the case of man's unity. "In both cases there would be something brought in from outside, making the person of Jesus doubly a juxtaposition of two realities, the divine nature being admittedly even far more heterogeneous than the human soul."[30]

Thus it seems that we are headed to the conclusion that Jesus was a mere man, an extraordinary man to be sure, but still purely and simply a man. Hulsbosch recognizes that this is a distinct risk in the approach that he takes, but he is anxious to avoid this conclusion. He believes that he can avoid it by insisting that Jesus is man in a new and higher way, so that through Jesus manhood has been brought to a new threshold and that Jesus himself has crossed over this threshold.[31] Hulsbosch also argues that Jesus is, as we are told in Colossians 1, 15, the "image of God." All men, of course, are the image of God, but Jesus is this image in a unique and superlative way. Thus Jesus as man is utterly unique; as the supreme image of God *he is* in a very real sense *the presence of God* to men and to the entire cosmos, and hence divine.[32] Yet Jesus, Hulsbosch insists, is this superlative image of God not in virtue of anything distinct from his humanity but precisely in virtue of his manhood: Jesus' character as revelation of God is, Hulsbosch affirms, "to be sought in Jesus' human subjectivity and not in a pre-existent divine person." Nevertheless the unique definitiveness of Jesus as man gives us grounds for affirming that he is as creature, man, and as revelation of God, truly God.[33]

Despite Hulsbosch's efforts to allow room for the genuine divinity of Jesus, it seems to me that the entire logic of his argument is opposed to this. At the beginning of this section, we noted that Hulsbosch had drawn parallels between the evolution of matter into living beings and the evolution of living beings into man. Hulsbosch himself argues that "the living being is not matter plus life but living matter. Man is not matter plus spirit but animated matter capable of those activities that we call spiritual." If we apply the same parallel to Jesus, it seems that we must conclude that "Jesus is not man plus God but divinized man." Although I certainly do not wish to say that "Jesus is man plus God" — for this would make any talk about his inner unity meaningless, I must confess that the thrust of Hulsbosch's thought seems to turn the traditional teaching about Jesus topsy-turvy. For in the tradition the great mystery of Christ is that in him *God has become man* whereas Hulsbosch seems to be saying that in Jesus *man has become God.* Perhaps this is not the intention behind Hulsbosch's way of approaching the unity of Jesus, but it seems to me to be the inescapable conclusion if we follow his arguments. This may be seen even more clearly if we look briefly at his teaching on the "preexistence" of Jesus, a theme that is taken up in more detail by his fellow Dutch theologian, Piet Schoonenberg.

Hulsbosch radically revises the notion of preexistence in his way of viewing the Christ event. According to traditional Christian teaching, as reflected in the prologue to John's Gospel, in the creeds, and in a constant line of development at the hands of theologians, the incarnation means that the eternal Word of the Father became flesh, and this Word was with God from the beginning,

from all eternity. And theologians have not hesitated in
saying that this eternal Word is a "person," distinct from
the Father from all eternity. For Hulsbosch, however,
Jesus' preexistence can be seen only as a kind of retro-
jection whereby we attribute an eternity to Jesus only
"after the fact," as it were. Because the man Jesus is
seen to be the supremely revelatory image of God, we
must, Hulsbosch argues, admit that this "divine dimension" of Jesus' being has existed from eternity. But it
exists from eternity only in the sense that the man Jesus
is anticipated by the personified Wisdom of God in fash-
ioning the universe, is mirrored by all of creation prior
to Jesus' actual physical existence, so that Jesus can
be said to be preexistent only to the extent that everything prior to him points toward him as the definitive revelation of God.[34] Whether this way of viewing Jesus' preexistence is correct or not can be left to the judgment
of Hulsbosch's peers; here it may be suggested, however,
that his position seems exceptionally difficult to reconcile with the prologue to John's Gospel and with the Christian tradition as a whole.

Perhaps the best way to conclude this section on Hulsbosch's attempt to reformulate the traditional faith of the
Church in Jesus along lines suggested by Teilhard's evolutionary world view is to offer the commentary on Hulsbosch's position given by the great Dominican theologian,
Edward Schillebeeckx. Schillebeeckx explicitly disavowed the evolutionary presuppositions behind Hulsbosch's
approach, and he took very serious exception to many
of the specific positions defended by Hulsbosch, in particular his rejection of the hypostatic union as a means
of safeguarding the unity of the divine and the human in
Jesus. Yet — and this is the major reason why it seems pertinent to append his evaluation to our report — Schillebeeckx
had a deep appreciation of what Hulsbosch was attempt-

ing to do. In giving his reasons for this appreciation, Schillebeeckx advances some suggestions of his own that are, I believe, immensely significant for us in our efforts to meditate on the mystery of Jesus. The substance of Schillebeeckx's view is as follows: ·

> Since 1953 I have firmly opposed the formulation "Christ is God and man," and also the confusing expression "the man Jesus is God." In this I was in the good company of Aquinas, for in his *Summa* (III, 16, 11, ad 1) he writes: "It is true that Christ, insofar as he is man, has the grace of union. But it is not true that Christ, insofar as he is man, is God." The proper formula would be: "Jesus Christ is the Son of God *in humanity*." The deepest sense of revelation is that God reveals himself in humanity. We cannot seek farther, above or beneath the man Jesus his being-God. The divinity must be perceptible *in* his humanity itself . . . . The human form of Jesus *is* the revelation of God. Expressions such as "Jesus besides being man is also God" evacuate the deepest meaning of the Incarnation. Christ could not be the revelation of God for us if *besides* the man Jesus we still needed a revelation of his divine nature − which in any case would then have to manifest itself in a *created* form . . . . We do not have present a man, Jesus, in whom is realized a presence of God which is distinct from him. The man Jesus *is* himself the presence of God . . . . If Christ is God, we know this only out of his mode of being man. It must be clear from his human situation: He must be man in a different and absolutely unique way.[35]

The value of Schillebeeckx's commentary, I believe, lies in the fact that it pinpoints the true value in Hulsbosch's approach. Schillebeeckx himself explicitly endorses the thought expressed in the title of Hulsbosch's article: "Jesus is known as man and is confessed to be the Son of God." For Schillebeeckx this means that the man Jesus and the incarnate Word are not two distinct realities: they are one, and we know the Word of God in

knowing the man Jesus. In many ways what Schillebeeckx
is saying here echoes a theme that we discovered when
we investigated the way in which Karl Rahner approaches
the mystery of Jesus. For Rahner the incarnation is the
mystery whereby the Word becomes flesh, God becomes
man. And since this becoming cannot take place within
God's inner triune life, it takes place in the reality that
he makes his own. God, who is unchangeable in himself, can
himself become subject to change *in something else,* namely
the created human reality of Jesus that he makes to be his
very own. Because this man Jesus has been made God's
very own reality, in knowing this man as man — so Schillebeeckx seems to be saying — we encounter God. We encounter God in the human reality of Jesus and not in any
reality distinct from this man Jesus.

Epilogue

What Does This All Mean?

If there is one common thread running through the contemporary discussion of the mystery of Jesus, it is a conviction that Christian people must take quite seriously and literally the truth, constantly affirmed throughout the history of Christianity yet seemingly little appreciated or understood, that Jesus is truly a man. All of the theologians discussed here do indeed acknowledge that Jesus was in some way divine; we may question quite legitimately whether some have succeeded in safeguarding this critical element in the Christian faith, for in some the explanation offered of Jesus' divinity seems in reality to explain away his character as true God. Yet all of the theologians represented here seem convinced that the most pernicious error in the history of Christian thought and the one most difficult to eradicate from popular understanding of Jesus is the tendency to look upon him as God dressed up like a man. Believers customarily give lip service to the truth that Jesus is truly man, but then we seem to forget all about it and to think of him exclusively in terms of his divinity. Here I believe that twentieth-century theologians are completely right. If we honestly ask ourselves how we view Jesus, and particularly if we ask our children how they look upon Jesus, we will probably discover that this is precisely how we do, in practice, understand the mystery of Christ. But this, contemporary theologians insist, is to misconceive radically the significance of the incarnation. It is to emasculate the Christian message and to rob of all meaning the fact that in Jesus God has truly become one of us, emptying himself of his divinity and sharing completely, totally, and personally our human condition.

All of this has profound repercussions on our way of viewing our own identity with Jesus and of understanding what he has achieved for us. Too often, I believe, we are disappointed because Jesus did not give us what many of us would really like to have: a rational explanation of the existence of suffering and agony and pain and frustration and death. We look on him exclusively as God, thinking that as God his suffering and death were different from ours, and that as God he could give us a reasonable answer to the problem of human suffering and death, and we complain that he does not. If we look at the Gospels we discover that Jesus did not promise us an answer to this mystery; he simply said that he, as Son of Man, had to suffer and that all who wished to become identified with him had to suffer too. But if we take Jesus' true humanity seriously, if we really mean it when we say that he is a man just as we are, then we can come to see how identification with Jesus is possible. According to the Gospels, Jesus' favorite way of referring to himself was to call himself the Son of Man, and he identified himself with the suffering servant portrayed in the songs of Isaiah. By doing this he emphasized that he was truly man, one of us, and that he experienced totally what it means to be a man. And precisely by becoming completely identified with us in our human condition, he has placed union with himself within the reach of all men. As John L. Mc-Kenzie puts it, those who identify themselves with Jesus cannot share his divine sonship except by adoption. But they can, he notes,

> share his human condition. Suffering and death are the normal human condition. Jesus does not ennoble them, but he makes them the means by which man is liberated from sin and death. Those who accept the human condition with him share in the redemptive act, the saving act of God. He demands nothing which is not within the reach of every man of every age. The ultimate futility in the life of unbelieving and hopeless man becomes the means of the ultimate fulfillment of the human potential. The deliverance of man is not to be accomplished by an act which can be shared by only a few. It is accomplished by perfect identity between Jesus and the race which he incorporates in himself. He meets man in the common destiny of all men.[1]

The quite ordinary life of Jesus, in other words, is the great stumbling block, the scandal of belief. To accept this scandal is to accept the mystery of the incarnation, the truly wondrous, paradoxical, completely unexpected gift of God's consuming love for men: his gift of himself in a created human reality that he has made his own and, in making it his own, has raised to life with himself.

Reflection on the incomprehensible love of God made incarnate in the suffering servant Jesus can, I hope, help us to appreciate what Paul meant when he exclaimed: "For I am certain of this: neither death nor life, no angel, no prince, nothing that exists, nothing still to come, not any power, or height or depth, nor any created thing, can ever come between us and the love of God made visible in Christ Jesus our Lord." (Romans 8:38-39). To grasp the full significance of these words, we must rid ourselves of any temptation to see Jesus as a mythical divine man or as a "god" walking on earth in the disguise of a man. We must be able to accept Jesus in his full humanity, seeing in this humanity an epiphany of the God who loves us so much that he asks us to love him in our fellowmen, even those we dislike and mistrust and envy and fear.

¹John L. McKenzie, *The Power and the Wisdom* (Milwaukee: Bruce, 1965), p. 102.

Bibliography

The following bibliography lists titles that I found particularly helpful in preparing this introductory report on Christ in contemporary thought. Since the footnotes provide details on the original writings of the theologians discussed, I have included here only those titles that seem best suited for an introductory acquaintance with their thought.

Chapter One. The Old and the New in Christology

De Rosa, Peter. *Christ and Original Sin.* Milwaukee: Bruce, 1967.

Robinson, John A. T. *Honest to God.* Philadelphia: Westminster, 1963.

Van de Pol, W. *The End of Conventional Christianity.* Glen Rock, N.J.: Paulist-Newman, 1968.

The special issue of *Commonweal* for November 24, 1967, entitled *Commonweal Papers*, No. 2. *Jesus*, is also particularly helpful for understanding the contemporary approach to Jesus. This has been reprinted in *God, Jesus, and the Spirit*, edited by Daniel Callahan, New York: Herder and Herder, 1969.

Chapter Two. Jesus and Contemporary Biblical Scholarship

Alonso Schokel, Luis. *Understanding Biblical Criticism*, New York: Herder and Herder, 1963.

Brown, Raymond. *New Testament Essays*. Milwaukee: Bruce, 1965. Reprinted as a Doubleday Image Book in 1968.

_____. *Jesus God and Man*. Milwaukee: Bruce, 1967.

Brown, Raymond and P. Joseph Cahill, *Biblical Tendencies today: An Introduction to the Post-Bultmannians*. Washing - ton: Corpus Papers, 1969.

Brown, Raymond, Joseph Fitzmyer, and Roland E. Murphy, editors, *The Jerome Biblical Commentary*. Englewood Cliffs, N.J.: Prentice-Hall, 1968. Two volumes in one. The essays in Volume II, The New Testament, on "Synoptic Problem" by Frederick Gast, "Modern New Testament Criticism" by John S. Kselman, and "Aspects of New Testament Thought" by David M. Stanley and Raymond Brown are particularly worth-while.

Bultmann, Rudolf. *Jesus and Mythology*. New York: Scribner's, 1958.

Cullmann, Oscar. *Christ and Time*. Philadelphia: Westminster, 1964 (rev. ed.).

_____. *The Christology of the New Testament*. Philadelphia: Westminster, 1963 (rev. ed.).

Fuller, Reginald. *A Critical Introduction to the New Testament*. London: Lutterworth, 1966.

_____. *Foundations of New Testament Christology*. New York: Scribner's, 1965.

McArthur, Harvey. *In Search of the Historical Jesus*. New York: Scribner's, 1969.

McKenzie, John L. *Dictionary of the Bible*. Milwaukee: Bruce, 1965. See in particular the articles on "Gospel," "Literary Forms," "Synoptic Question," and on the individual Gospels.

_____. *The Power and the Wisdom*. Milwaukee. Bruce, 1965.

Quesnell, Quentin. *This Good News: An Introduction to the Catholic Theology of the New Testament*. Milwaukee: Bruce, 1964.

Robinson, James M. *The New Quest for the Historical Jesus*. London: SCM Press, 1959.

Chapter Three. Jesus and Speculative Theology

Good introductions to Barth, Tillich, and Bonhoeffer are found in the following surveys of contemporary Protestant thought:

Curtis, C. A. *Contemporary Protestant Thought*. New York: Bruce, 1970.

Marty, Martin and Dean Peerman, editors. *A Handbook of Christian Theologians*. Cleveland: World, 1964.

Hunt, George L. *Ten Makers of Modern Protestant Thought*. New York: Association Press, 1958.

For Barth see

Barth, Karl. *Church Dogmatics: A Selection*, edited by Helmut Gollwitzer. New York: Harper Torchbooks, 1962.

_____. *Evangelical Theology: An Introduction*. New York: Holt, Rinehart & Winston, 1963.

O'Grady, Colm. *A Survey of the Theology of Karl Barth*. New York: Corpus Papers, 1970.

For Tillich see

Tillich, Paul. *Systematic Theology* (3 volumes in one). Chicago: University of Chicago Press, 1965. Volume I was published originally in 1953, Volume II in 1957, and Volume III in 1962.

Ambruster, Carl. *The Vision of Paul Tillich.* New York: Sheed & Ward, 1966.

Brown, D. MacKenzie. *Ultimate Concern: Paul Tillich in Dialogue.* New York: Harper & Row, 1965.

O'Meara, Thomas and Celestin Weisser, editors. *Paul Tillich in Catholic Thought.* Dubuque, Iowa: Priory Press, 1964.

For Bonhoeffer see

Bonhoeffer, Dietrich. *Christ the Center.* New York: Harper & Row, 1966.

_____. *Ethics.* New York: Macmillan, 1965 paperback edition.

_____. *Cost of Discipleship.* New York: Macmillan, 1966 paperback edition.

_____. *Letters and Papers from Prison.* New York: Macmillan, 1962.

Kuhns, William. *In Pursuit of Dietrich Bonhoeffer.* Dayton, Ohio: Pflaum, 1968. Reprinted in a Doubleday Image book edition in 1969.

Marty, Martin, editor. *The Place of Bonhoeffer.* New York: Association Press, 1962.

For Pannenberg see

Pannenberg, Wolfhart. *Jesus: God and Man.* Philadelphia: Westminster, 1968.

Robinson, James M. and John Cobb, Jr., editors. *Theology as History*. New York: Harper & Row, 1967.

For Rahner see

Rahner, Karl. Articles "Incarnation" and "Jesus Christ. IV. History of Dogma and Theology" in *Sacramentum Mundi*, Vol. III. New York: Herder and Herder, 1969.

——————————. "On the Theology of the Incarnation," *Theological Investigations*, Vol. 4. Baltimore: Helicon, 1966.

Vorgrimler, Herbert. *Karl Rahner: His Life, Thought and Works*. Glen Rock, New Jersey: Paulist Deus Books, 1963.

Roberts, Louis. *The Achievement of Karl Rahner*. New York: Herder and Herder, 1967.

Chapter Four: Jesus in an Evolutionary World View

Du Lubac, Henri. *Teilhard de Chardin: The Man and His Meaning*. New York: Hawthorn, 1965.

North, Robert. *In Search of the Human Jesus*. New York: Corpus Papers, 1970. This is a revised version of the two articles by North mentioned in the notes for Chapter Four in which he surveys the views of Hulsbosch and others.

Pittenger, Norman. *Christology Reconsidered*. London: SCM Press, 1970.

Footnotes

Footnotes Chapter 1

[1]Regin Prenter, *Creation and Redemption* (Philadelphia: Fortress, 1967), pp. 292 ff., offers very illuminating insights on this question.

[2]Norman Pittenger, *Christology Reconsidered* (London: SCM Press, 1970), p. 7.

[3]The "Apostles' Creed" was fixed early in the third century at Rome. Originally it was developed for liturgical use as a profession of baptismal faith. The creed recited at Mass is usually referred to as the "Nicene Creed," but in fact this Creed includes some additions to the formulas found in the Creed proclaimed at the Council of Nicea in 325. Popularly it is known as the "Nicene-Constantinople Creed," inasmuch as it was stated in the form in which it is now recited at the Council of Constantinople in 381. However some scholars maintain that this is not exactly correct. For a discussion of these Creeds see the article "Creeds" by Pierre-Thomas Camelot in *Sacramentum Mundi* (New York: Herder and Herder, 1968), 2: 37-40.

[4]The passages in the first epistle of John 4, 2 and in the second epistle of John 7 are considered by contemporary scholars as directed against early docetists. In these passages the bodily reality of Jesus is stressed, in particular the fact that he had a real flesh that could be seen and touched.

[5]Ignatius of Antioch, *Letter to the Trallians* 9-10, translated by K..Lake in the Loeb Classical Library.

[6]Clement of Alexandria as cited by James M. Carmody and Thomas E. Clarke, eds., *Word and Redeemer* (Glen Rock, N.J.: Paulist Press, 1966), p. 27.

[7]Cf. note 3.

[8]Peter de Rosa, *Christ and Original Sin* (Milwaukee: Bruce, 1967), p. 3.

[9]*Ibid.*, p. 4.

[10]Raymond E. Brown, *Jesus, God and Man* (Milwaukee: Bruce, 1968), pp. 39-102, offers a superb analysis of the pertinent biblical texts relative to the subject of Jesus' human knowledge. He takes up four major points: Jesus' knowledge about ordinary affairs of life; his knowledge of the future; his knowledge of religious matters; and his understanding of himself and his mission. Brown's study is very important for anyone who is anxious to know in some detail how the gospels describe the human knowledge of Jesus.

[11]The Council of Chaldedon in 451 was the last of several Councils dealing with the question of Jesus' divinity and, more particularly, with the interrelation of the divine and the human in Jesus. Its formulation of the latter relationship reads as follows: "We acknowledge one and the same Lord Jesus Christ . . . in two natures without confusion, without change, without division, without separation — the difference of the natures being by no means taken away because of the union, but rather the distinctive character of each nature being preserved, and each combining in one Person and *hypostasis* — not divided or separated into two Persons, but one and the same Son and only-begotten God, Word, Lord Jesus Christ . . . ."

[12]Karl Rahner, "Current Problems in Christology," in *Theological Investigations* (Baltimore: Helicon, 1961), 1 : 156-157.

[13]John A. T. Robinson, *Honest to God* (Philadelphia: Westminster, 1963). p. 65.

[14]*Ibid.*, p. 66.

[15]Rahner, "Current Problems in Christology," p. 155.

[16]Raymond E. Brown, "Resurrection and Biblical Criticism," in *Commonweal Papers: II, Jesus* (November 24, 1967), 234.

[17]*Ibid.*, 234.

[18]An excellent introductory work on contemporary biblical criticism, particularly for the way in which the New Testament is understood by biblical scholars today, is Quentin Quesnell's *This Good News: An Introduction to the Catholic Theology of the New Testament* (Milwaukee: Bruce, 1965). A brief and very helpful summary is found in John L. McKenzie's *Dictionary of the Bible* (Milwaukee: Bruce, 1965), article "Gospel," pp. 320-323.

[19]See, for example, the arguments advanced by Leslie Dewart in his *The Future of Belief* (New York: Herder and Herder, 1966) and *The Foundations of Belief* (New York: Herder and Herder, 1969). A popular presentation of his views is given by Dewart in *Spectrum of Catholic Attitudes*, edited by Robert Campbell (Milwaukee: Bruce, 1969).

[20]A handy resume of Hamilton's views, and in particular his understanding of the meaning of "nature" and "person" as used in the Chalcedonian decrees is given by him in his article "Good-by Chalcedon, Hello What?" in *Commonweal Papers: II: Jesus* (November 24, 1967). One of the theologians who, in the same Commonweal Paper, had attempted to construct his thought on the basis of the Chalcedonian decrees, Frederick Crowe, was mentioned somewhat condescendingly by Hamilton in the course of his essay. Crowe replied to Hamilton, severely criticizing him for attacking something that he did not understand in an article "Christologies: How Up to Date is Yours?" in *Theological Studies,* September, 1968.

Footnotes Chapter 2

[1]On the meaning of the title "Lord" in the New Testament see John L. McKenzie, *Dictionary of the Bible* (Milwaukee: Bruce, 1965), art. "Lord," pp. 516-518; Oscar Cullmann, *The Christology of the New Testament* (rev. ed., Philadelphia: Westminster, 1963), pp. 195-237.

[2]On the chronological priority of the Pauline epistles to the written Gospels, see R. H. Fuller, *A Critical Introduction to the New Testament* (London: Lutterworth, 1966), ch. 2. For a shorter discussion, see George T. Montague, *The Living*

Thought of St. Paul (Contemporary College Theology Series) (Milwaukee: Bruce, 1966), pp. 1-11.

[3] On the Christological hymns in Paul and their probable origin in liturgical celebrations see D. M. Stanley, "Carmenque Christo quasi Deo Dicere" in *Catholic Biblical Quarterly* 20 (1958): 173-191.

[4] For a very interesting discussion of the "kingdom" or "reign" of God and what it signifies, see John L. McKenzie, *The Power and the Wisdom* (Milwaukee: Bruce, 1965), pp. 48-70.

[5] On Jesus' own use of the title "Messiah" or "Christ" see Cullmann, *The Christology of the New Testament*, pp. 117-133, and Raymond E. Brown, *Jesus, God and Man* (Milwaukee: Bruce, 1967), pp. 79-86.

[6] On Jesus' personal preference for the title "Son of Man," see the very interesting development provided by John L. McKenzie in *The Power and the Wisdom*, pp. 90-107.

[7] The way in which Jesus himself seems to have linked the concept of "Son of Man" to the enigmatic "Suffering Servant of Yahweh" is discussed by McKenzie in the same section of his *The Power and the Wisdom* to which we referred in the previous note. McKenzie's articles on "Servant of the Lord" (pp. 791-794) and on "Son of Man" (pp. 831-833) in his *Dictionary of the Bible* provide very useful summaries for the meaning attached to these terms in the New Testament, particularly for the way in which Jesus himself seemingly utilized them to convey to his disciples that his messianic role was far different from the role that contemporary Judaism had assigned to the Messiah.

[8] The German edition of Schweitzer's work, *Von Reimarus zu Wrede*, was published in 1906. Apparently the title given to the English translation was a poetic rendering of the German subtitle, which ran "A History of Research upon the Life of Jesus."

[9] Reimarus' work, from which only excerpts were published after his death, was called *On the Intention of Jesus and His Disciples (Von dem Zweck Jesu und seinen Junger).*

[10] James M. Robinson, *A New Quest of the Historical Jesus* (London: SCM Press, 1959), p. 26.

[11]Because of recent discoveries, among them the Johns Rylands papyrus containing a passage from the Gospel according to John and of very ancient age and the light that the Dead Sea Scrolls have cast on the mentality and intellectual movements current in the Judaism of Jesus' time, scholars today are much more ready to acknowledge the historical value of the Fourth Gospel than they were during the nineteenth century. However, many contemporary scholars are still quite reluctant to concede a great deal of value to this Gospel as a reliable historical source. Perhaps the best contemporary biblical expert on the Johannine literature, Raymond E. Brown, however, believes that biblical scholars should be more open to the historical value of this Gospel. Brown discusses the basic problem of the historicity of John in his *New Testament Essays* (Milwaukee: Bruce, 1965), pp. 143-167.

[12]Harvey K. McArthur, *In Search of the Historical Jesus* (New York: Scribner's, 1969), p. 5.

[13]Kähler's work, called *Der sogennante historische Jesus und der geschichtliche, biblische Christus,* was first published in Germany in 1892; a second edition appeared in 1896, and it was reissued in 1928, with the latest printing being in 1956. His work did not exercise its full influence when it was first published; in fact for a long time it apparently went unnoticed, for it is not mentioned in Schweitzer's famous book on the nineteenth-century quest. However, it has recently been translated into English by Carl E. Braaten and introduced into the English-speaking world with a foreword by Paul Tillich (Philadelphia: Fortress, 1964).

[14]The words "kerygma" and "kerygmatic," which appear quite frequently in contemporary biblical literature, are derived from a Greek word for "proclamation" or "preaching."

[15]This distinction is not quite as clear in English as it is in German, where two entirely different words are used. In German "historical," or purely objective factual history, is *"historisch"* (derived from a noun *Historie*), whereas "historic," or the significant or meaningful in history, is *"geschichtliche"* (derived from a noun *Geschichte*).

[16]The original German title was *Das Messiasgeheimnis in den Evangelien.*

[17] James M. Robinson, *A New Quest of the Historical Jesus* p. 35.

[18] Here the major work of Dodd is his *The Apostolic Preaching* (New York: Harper, 1936). In it he suggests that it is possible to distinguish a central kerygma in the New Testament, possibly represented by the sermons in Acts, that is an outline not only of Jesus' teaching but also an historical sketch of his ministry.

[19] Raymond E. Brown, "After Bultmann, What?" in *Biblical Tendencies Today* (Washington: Corpus Papers, 1969), p. 6.

[20] James M. Robinson, *A New Quest of the Historical Jesus*, pp. 28-29; see also pp. 66-72 where Robinson defends the legitimacy of a "new quest" on the basis that today there is operative a new concept or understanding both of history and of the self than there was during the nineteenth century.

[21] Raymond E. Brown, "After Bultmann, What?" pp. 18, 20, 21.

[22] John L. McKenzie, article "Literary Forms" in *Dictionary of the Bible*, p. 513.

[23] *Ibid.*, p. 514.

[24] John Macquarrie, "Rudolf Bultmann," in *A Handbook of Christian Theologians*, edited by Martin E. Marty and Dean G. Peerman (Cleveland: World, 1965), p. 445.

[25] Rudolf Bultmann, *Glauben und Verstehen*, Vol. 1, pp. 204, 265.
[26] *Ibid.*
[27] *Ibid.*, p. 266.
[28] Rudolf Bultmann, *Jesus and the Word* (New York: Scribner's, 1934), p. 8
[29] Rudolf Bultmann, *Jesus and Mythology* (New York: Scribner's, 1958), p. 16.
[30] Bultmann, *Glauben und Verstehen*, Vol. 1, pp. 265-266.
[31] Bultmann, "The New Testament and Mythology," in *Kerygma and Myth*, edited by H. W. Bartsch (New York: Harper, 1953) Vol. I, p. 35.
[32] Bultmann, *Jesus and Mythology*, p. 12.

[33]*Ibid.*, pp. 14-15.

[34]*Ibid.*, p. 17.

[35]Bultmann, "The New Testament and Mythology," p. 5.

[36]See *Ibid.*, p. 45, and Rudolf Bultmann, *History of the Synoptic Tradition* (New York: Harper, 1963), p. 308.

[37]Bultmann, "The New Testament and Mythology," p. 10, n. 2.

[38]Bultmann, *Jesus and Mythology*, p. 15.

[39]*Ibid.*, p. 45. See also "The Problem of Hermeneutics," in *Essays, Philosophical and Theological* (New York: Macmillan, 1955), pp. 234-261.

[40]Bultmann, *Jesus and Mythology*, p. 43.

[41]*Ibid.*

[42]Leopold Malevez, *The Christian Message and Myth* (Westminster, Md.: Newman, 1958), p. 156.

[43]For a good presentation of Bultmann's relationship to Heidegger see John Macquarrie, *An Existentialist Theology: A Comparison of Heidegger and Bultmann* (New York: Harper Torchbooks, 1965).

[44]Bultmann, *Jesus and Mythology*, p. 23.

[45]*Ibid.*, p. 26.

[46]Rudolf Bultmann, *The Presence of Eternity* (New York: Harper, 1957), p. 155 (in England the work was published under the title *History and Eschatology*).

[47]John Macquarrie, "Rudolf Bultmann," p. 454.

[48]Rudolf Bultmann, *The Theology of the New Testament* (New York: Scribner's, 1951), Vol. I, p. 8.

[49]Bultmann, *Jesus and Mythology*, pp. 79-80.

[50]In "The New Testament and Mythology," p. 7, Bultmann declares: "What a primitive mythology it is that a divine being should become incarnate and atone for the sins of men through his own blood!"

[51]*Ibid.*, p. 46.

[52]Here see André Malet, *Mythos et Logos: La Pensée de Rudolf Bultmann* (Geneva: Librairie Protestante, 1962), pp. 377-385.

[53]Macquarrie, "Rudolf Bultmann," p. 455.

[54]*Glauben und Verstehen*, Vol. II, p. 258.

[55]*Ibid.*, Vol. I, p. 334.

[56]Raymond E. Brown, "After Bultmann, What?" pp. 1-2.

[57]Oscar Cullmann, *Christ and Time* (revised ed. Philadelphia: Westminster, 1964), p. xii.

[58]Oscar Cullmann, *Salvation in History* (New York: Harper & Row, 1967), p. 192.

[59]See Cullmann, *Christ and Time*, p. 121 ff.

[60]*Ibid.*, p. 124.

[61]*Ibid.*, p. 127.

[62] Oscar Cullmann, *The Christology of the New Testament* (revised edition, Philadelphia: Westminster, 1963), pp. 1-2.

[63]*Ibid.*, pp. 3-4.

[64]*Ibid.*, p. 4.

[65]*Ibid.*, p. 5. See also *ibid.*, p. 316, where Cullmann writes: "The variety which results from the plurality of the Christological titles and solutions; the discovery that each of the temporally different Christological functions can first of all be the object of a particular title; the discovery that connection with other titles only gradually appears, and that with it a perspective of *Heilsgeschichte* arises — all this proves that the question about Jesus was not answered by early Christianity in terms of a mythology already at hand, but in terms of a series of real facts. These facts were events which happened in the first century of our era, facts which were unnoticed by those who at that time 'made history' and which today can still be interpreted differently, but are not for this reason less historical. They are the events of the life, work, and death of Jesus of Nazareth, and the experience of his presence and continuing work beyond death within the fellowship of his disciples."

[66]*Ibid.*, p. 306.

[67]*Ibid.*, pp. 324-325.

[68]*Ibid.*, p. 321.

[69]*Salvation in History*, pp. 287-288.

[70]*The Christology of the New Testament*, p. 321.

[71]*Ibid.*, p. 325.

[72]*Salvation in History*, p. 321.

[73]*Ibid.*, pp. 320-321.

[74] On this point it is also useful to consult Cullmann's "Out of Season Remarks on the 'Historical Jesus' of the Bultmann School," in Harvey K. McArthur, editor, *In Search of the Historical Jesus* (New York: Scribner's, 1969), pp. 259-280.

Footnotes Chapter 3

[1] On this, see the introduction to the second edition of *The Epistle to the Romans* (Oxford: Oxford University Press, 1933). Also see Thomas Torrance, "Karl Barth," *Ten Makers of Modern Protestant Thought*, edited by George L. Hunt (New York: Association Press, 1958), pp. 60-62.

[2] Karl Barth, *Evangelical Theology: An Introduction* (New York: Holt, Rinehart & Winston, 1963), p. 6.

[3]*Ibid.*, p. 11. Cf. Karl Barth, *Church Dogmatics* (hereafter abbreated CD) IV, 1 (The Doctrine of Reconciliation) (Edinburgh: T. & T. Clark, 1956), pp. 187-188. The text is found

in *Church Dogmatics: A Selection* (New York: Harper Torch-books, 1962), pp. 112-114.

⁴CD, II, 2 (The Doctrine of God) (Edinburgh: T. & T. Clark, 1957), p. 94. Text in *Church Dogmatics: A Selection*, p. 110.

⁵On this see *Church Dogmatics*, I, 2 (The Doctrine of the Word of God) (Edinburgh: T. & T. Clark, 1956), p. 123. See also Colm O'Grady, *The Church in the Theology of Karl Barth* (Washington: Corpus, 1969), p. 75.

⁶CD, IV, 2 (The Doctrine of Reconciliation) (Edinburgh: T. & T. Clark, 1958), p. 50. In *A Selection*, p. 45.

⁷See O'Grady, *The Church in the Theology of Karl Barth*, p. 133.

⁸CD, IV, 1, p. 161. In *A Selection*, p. 94.

⁹Barth, *Evangelical Theology*, p. 28.

¹⁰*Ibid.*, pp. 29-30. "A twofold Jesus Christ," Barth adds, "one who existed *before* and another who existed *after* Easter, can be deduced from New Testament texts only after he has been arbitrarily read into them." *Ibid.*, p. 30. Cf. CD, IV, 2, p. 247 *(A Selection*, p. 120).

¹¹On the astonishment or wonder characteristic of a theology centered on Immanuel, the God with us, see Barth, *Evangelical Theology*, pp. 70-71.

¹²CD, IV, 1, pp. 183-184. In *A Selection*, pp. 112-113.

¹³CD, IV, 1, p. 127.

¹⁴CD, IV, 1, p. 127.

¹⁵CD, IV, 1, pp. 34-39.

¹⁶CD, IV, 1, p. 53.

¹⁷CD, IV, 1, p. 50 *(A Selection*, p. 45).

¹⁸CD, IV, 1, pp. 179-181.

¹⁹CD, IV, 1, p. 186.

²⁰CD, IV, 1, pp. 186-187 *(A Selection*, pp. 113-114).

²¹CD, IV, 1, pp. 81-82.

²²See Karl Barth, *Christ and Adam* (New York: Collier, 1962), pp. 12-14, 38-42.

²³CD, IV, 2, p. 27.

²⁴CD, IV, 2, pp. 44-50.

²⁵CD, IV, 2, p. 59.

²⁶CD, IV, 2, pp. 91-92.

²⁷CD, I, 2, p. 136.

²⁸CD, IV, 2, p. 98.

²⁹CD, IV, 2, pp. 109-112.

³⁰CD, IV, 3 (Edinburgh: T. & T. Clark, 1961), p. 44.

³¹CD, IV, 3, p. 99 *(A Selection*, p. 230).

³²See Robert Clyde Johnson, "Paul Tillich," in *Ten Makers of Modern Protestant Thought*, edited by George L. Hunt (New York: Association Press, 1958), p. 91.

[33] Paul Tillich, *Systematic Theology* (Chicago: University of Chicago Press, 1953), I, p. 61. (Hereafter this will be abbreviated ST. Volume II appeared in 1957 and Volume III in 1961).

[34] ST, I, p. 61.

[35] ST, I, p. 62.

[36] Paul Tillich, *Dynamics of Faith* (New York: Harper, 1958), pp. 41-54.

[37] ST, I, p. 235.

[38] Tillich, *Dynamics of Faith*, p. 42.

[39] *Ibid.*

[40] *Ibid.*, p. 43.

[41] Letter to Gustave Weigel and found in the reprint of Weigel's article, "The Theological Significance of Paul Tillich, " in *Paul Tillich in Catholic Thought*, edited by Thomas A. O' Meara and Celestin D. Weisser (Dubuque, Iowa: Priory Press, 1964), p. 23.

[42] ST, I, p. 189.

[43] Paul Tillich, *Love, Power, and Justice* (New York: Oxford University Press, 1960), p. 38.

[44] Paul Tillich, *The Courage to Be* (New Haven, Conn.: Yale University Press, 1952), p. 35.

[45] *Ultimate Concern: Paul Tillich in Dialogue*, edited by D. MacKenzie Brown (New York: Harper & Row, 1965), p. 45.

[46] ST, I, p. 203.

[47] ST, II, pp. 44-45.

[48] See Johnson, "Paul Tillich," pp. 94-95.

[49] See Tillich, *Love, Power, and Justice*, p. 25.

[50] ST, II, p. 97.

[51] ST, II, p. 94.

[52] ST, II, 142.

[53] ST, II, 142.

[54] ST, II, 147-148.

[55] ST, II, pp. 97-98.

[56] ST, II, p. 99.

[57] Brown, ed., *Ultimate Concern*, p. 133.

[58] *Ibid.*, pp. 146-147.

[59] ST, II, p. 107.

[60] ST, II, p. 149.

[61] ST, II, p. 94.

[62] See above, p. 55

[63] ST, II, p. 148.

[64] Paul Tillich, "A Reinterpretation of the Doctrine of the Incarnation" *Church Quarterly Review* 147 (January, 1949), 143.

[65] Paul Tillich, *The Eternal Now* (New York: Scribner's, 1963), p. 76.

[66] ST, II, p. 119.

[67] ST, II, p. 166.

[68] Cited by Reinhold Niebuhr, *Union Theological Seminary Quarterly Review* 1, no. 3 (March, 1956), 3.

[69] Found in Dietrich Bonhoeffer, *No Rusty Swords* (New York: Harper & Row, 1965), p. 68.

[70] Dietrich Bonhoeffer, *Ethics* (New York: Macmillan, 1955; paperback ed. 1965), pp. 33-34.

[71] Dietrich Bonhoeffer, *Christ the Center* (New York: Harper & Row, 1966), p. 75.

[72] *Ibid.*

[73] *Ibid.*, p. 91.

[74] *Ibid.*, p. 32.

[75] *Ibid.*, pp. 31-34.

[76] *Ibid.*, p. 107.

[77] *Ibid.*, p. 108.

[78] *Ibid.*, p. 111.

[79] *Ibid.*, pp. 112-113.

[80] *Ibid.*, p. 116.

[81] *Ibid.*, pp. 47-48.

[82] Dietrich Bonhoeffer, *Communion of Saints* (New York: Harper & Row, 1964), p. 100.

[83] *Ibid.*, p. 106.

[84] *Ibid.*, p. 107.

[85] Dietrich Bonhoeffer, *Act and Being* (New York: Harper & Row, 1963), p. 90.

[86] *Ibid.*, p. 121.

[87] Bonhoeffer, *Christ the Center*, p. 51.

[88] Dietrich Bonhoeffer, *The Cost of Discipleship* (New York: Macmillan, 1966), p. 7.

[89] *Ibid.*, p. 63.

[90] *Ibid.*, p. 211.

[91] Bonhoeffer, *Ethics*, p. 144.

[92] *Ibid.*, p. 145.

[93] Dietrich Bonhoeffer, *Letters and Papers from Prison* (New York: Macmillan, 1962), p. 154.

[94] *Ibid.*, p. 156.

[95] *Ibid.*, p. 219.

[96] *Ibid.*, p. 219.

[97] *Ibid.*, p. 175. See pp. 164-165.

[98] *Ibid.*, pp. 209-210.

[99] Bonhoeffer, *Christ the Center*, p. 62.

[100] *Ibid.*

101 Dietrich Bonhoeffer, *Life Together* (New York: Harper & Row, 1954), p. 108.

102 James M. Robinson, "Revelation in Word and History," in *Theology as History*, edited by James M. Robinson and John B. Cobb, Jr. (New York: Harper & Row, 1967), notes on pages 97-100 that Pannenberg has been exceptionally well received by American Protestant groups alarmed over the liberalism of Bultmann and his followers and anxious for a more literal and "orthodox" approach to theological issues. Whether these groups have been correct in seizing upon Pannenberg as their champion will become clearer toward the conclusion of this section on Pannenberg.

103 Wolfhart Pannenberg, *Jesus: God and Man* (Philadelphia: Westminster, 1968), p. 19.

104 *Ibid.*, p. 130.

105 *Ibid.*, p. 30.

106 Pannenberg, "Response to Discussion," in *Theology as History*, p. 232.

107 *Ibid.* Emphasis added.

108 Pannenberg, *Offenbarung als Geschichte* (Göttingen: Vandenboeck und Ruprecht, 1961, 2nd ed., 1963), p. 17. Cited in Robinson, "Revelation in Word and History," p. 63.

109 Pannenberg, "Response to Discussion," pp. 239-240. Robinson, in his "Revelation in Word and History," pp. 63-64, lists several major thesis on revelation that Pannenberg proposes as presuppositions to theological inquiry in his *Offenbarung als Geschichte*.

110 Pannenberg, *Jesus: God and Man*, p. 388.

111 *Ibid.*, p. 129.

112 *Ibid.*, pp. 53-66.

113 *Ibid.*, p. 99.

114 Pannenberg, "The Revelation of God in Jesus," pp. 128-129.

115 Pannenberg, *Jesus: God and Man*, p. 98.

116 *Ibid.*, p. 97.

117 *Ibid.*, p. 105.

118 *Ibid.*, pp. 129-130.

119 *Ibid.*, p. 127.

120 *Ibid.*, p. 159.

121 *Ibid.*, p. 332.

122 *Ibid.*, p. 378 f. Cf. p. 390.

123 *Ibid.*, p. 367.

124 *Ibid.*, p. 395.

125 *Ibid.*, pp. 396-397.

126 *Ibid.*, pp. 395-396.

127 Pannenberg, "Response to Discussion," p. 232.

[128]This is a citation from John B. Cobb, Jr., in a feature review of Pannenberg's *Jesus: God and Man* in *The Journal of Religion* 49 (April, 1969), 200. The citation is intended by Cobb to summarize Pannenberg's doctrine of God, which is set forth explicitly in his *Was ist Der Mensch?* This work of Pannenberg was published in 1970 by Fortress Press under the title *What Is Man?*

[129]The principal sources for Rahner's teaching on Jesus are the following: "Current Problems in Christology," *Theological Investigations*, Vol. I (Baltimore: Helicon, 1961) (referred to as "Current Problems . . ."), "On the Theology of the Incarnation," *Theological Investigations*, Vol. IV (Baltimore: Helicon, 1966) (referred to as "Incarnation"); "Dogmatic Reflections on the Knowledge and Self-Consciousness of Christ," *Theological Investigations*, Vol. V (Baltimore: Helicon, 1966) (referred to as "Dogmatic Reflections . . ."); "Incarnation," *Sacramentum Mundi*, Vol. 3 (New York: Herder and Herder, 1969) (referred to as "Incarnation," SM); and "Jesus Christ: IV. History of Dogma and Theology," *Sacramentum Mundi*, Vol. 3 (referred to as "Jesus Christ . . .").

[130]"Incarnation," SM, 110.

[131]*Ibid.*, 113.

[132]"Jesus Christ . . . ," 196. See "Current Problems . . . ," p. 150.

[133]"Current Problems . . . ," p. 165.

[134]Karl Rahner, "On the Theology of Symbol," *Theological Investigations* (Baltimore: Helicon, 1966), Vol. IV, pp. 226-227.

[135]*Ibid.*, p. 225.

[136]*Ibid.*, p. 236.

[137]"Incarnation," SM, 114.

[138]*Ibid.*, 114-115.

[139]"Jesus Christ . . . ," 206.

[140]*Ibid.*, 196.

[141]*Ibid.*, 206.

[142]"Dogmatic Reflections . . . , " pp. 193-194.

[143]*Ibid.*, p. 203.

[144]*Ibid.*, pp. 200-201.

[145]*Ibid.*, p. 205.

[146]*Ibid.*, p. 207.

[147]*Ibid.*, pp. 207-208; emphasis added.

[148]*Ibid.*, p. 209.

[149]Karl Rahner and Herbert Vorgrimler, *Dictionary of Theology* (New York: Herder and Herder, 1965), p. 240.

[150]See "Incarnation," p. 107; "Incarnation," SM, 115-116.

[151] "Incarnation," pp. 109-110.
[152] *Ibid.*, p. 113, see also p. 115.
[153] *Ibid.*, p. 115.
[154] *Ibid.*, p. 116.
[155] *Ibid.*
[156] *Ibid.*, p. 117.
[157] "Jesus Christ...," 196. See "Death,"*Sacramentum Mundi* Vol. 2 (New York: Herder and Herder, 1968), 58. See also Rahner's *Toward a Theology of Death* (New York: Herder and Herder, 1966).
[158] "Death," *Sacramentum Mundi,* 61.
[159] "Incarnation," pp. 116-117.
[160] "Jesus Christ...," 194; "Incarnation," p. 119.
[161] "Jesus Christ...," 194-195.

Footnotes Chapter 4

[1] Norman Pittenger, "Process Theology," in *Dictionary of Christian Theology,* edited by Alan Richardson (Philadelphia: Westminster, 1969), p. 275.
[2] Norman Pittenger, *Christology Reconsidered* (London: SCM Press, 1970), pp. 121-123.
[3] *Ibid.*, p. 123.
[4] *Ibid.*, p. 47. See also pp. 56-67.
[5] *Ibid.*, pp. 67-68.
[6] *Ibid.*, p. 128.
[7] *Ibid.*, pp. 55-56.
[8] *Ibid.*, pp. 74-75.
[9] *Ibid.*, p. 78. See pp. 76-77.
[10] *Ibid.*, p. 96.
[11] Pittenger holds that although Christian thought has indeed affirmed the true manhood of Jesus in word, it has hardly been successful in making this affirmation meaningful in creative and imaginative understanding. "During the history of the Christian community," he writes, "there has always been a tendency to emphasize the divinity in such a fashion that the humanity has been minimized." *Ibid.*, pp. 9-10.
[12] *Ibid.*, p. 114.
[13] *Ibid.*, p. 119.
[14] *Ibid.*
[15] *Ibid.*
[16] *Ibid.*, p. 141.
[17] *Ibid.*, p. 142.
[18] *Ibid.* Emphasis added.
[19] *Ibid.*
[20] For Teilhard's teaching on the "without" and "within" of matter see his *Phenomenon of Man* (New York: Harper &

Row, 1959), pp. 52-55.

[21]The foregoing section on Teilhard has been an effort to summarize as accurately as possible the position outlined in his *Phenomenon of Man*. Good introductions to Teilhard are: Henri de Lubac, *Teilhard de Chardin: The Man and His Work* (New York: Hawthorn, 1965); Joseph Koob, *Teilhard de Chardin: A New Synthesis of Evolution* (New York: Paulist Press, 1965), very simple yet a clear introduction. For Teilhard's view on man see Robert North, *Teilhard and the Creation of the Soul* (Milwaukee: Bruce, 1966); for the centrality of Christ in Teilhard's thought see Christopher Mooney, *Teilhard de Chardin and the Mystery of Christ* (New York: Harper & Row, 1966; reprinted as a Doubleday Image Book, 1969).

[22]The articles by Hulsbosch, Schillebeeckx, and Schoonenberg appeared in a special issue of the *Tijdschrift voor Theologie 6* (1966). Hulsbosch's article, pp. 250-273, was entitled "Jezus Christus, gekend als mens, beleden as Zoon Gods"; Schillebeeckx', pp. 274-288, was called "Persoonlijke openbaringsgestalte van de Vader"; and Schoonenberg's, pp. 289-306, was called "Christus zonder tweeheid?" The three articles were given almost complete summation by Robert North in a superb article, "Soul-Body Unity and God-Man Unity" in *Theological Studies* 30 (March, 1969), pp. 27-60. North also reported on their position in an article "Recent Christology and Theological Method" in *Continuum* 7 (Winter-Spring, 1969), pp. 63-77. Throughout this section I have used the translations provided by North in this *Theological Studies* article, and although I give the page for the original Dutch articles I add in parentheses the page number of North's article reporting on the Dutch discussion.

[23]Hulsbosch, p. 250 (North, p. 30).
[24]*Ibid.*, p. 251 (North, p. 31).
[25]*Ibid.*, p. 251 (North, p. 28).
[26]North, p. 27, paraphrasing Hulsbosch.
[27]*Ibid.*, p. 252 (North, p. 32).
[28]*Ibid.*, p. 255 (North, pp. 36-37).
[29]*Ibid.*, p. 254 (North, p. 33).
[30]North, p. 33.
[31]Hulsbosch, p. 254 (North, pp. 33-34).
[32]*Ibid.*, p. 261 (North, p. 44).
[33]*Ibid.*, pp. 265-266 (North, p. 46).
[34]*Ibid.*, pp. 266-267 (North, p. 47).
[35]Schillebeeckx, pp. 276-277 (North, pp. 40-41).

INDEX